Woody Durham

A Tar Heel Voice

*Darrell —
Thanks for listening!
Woody Durham*

Woody Durham
A Tar Heel Voice

by Woody Durham with Adam Lucas

JOHN F. BLAIR, PUBLISHER
Winston-Salem, North Carolina

Published by
JOHN F. BLAIR,
PUBLISHER
1406 Plaza Drive
Winston-Salem, North Carolina 27103
www.blairpub.com

COVER PHOTOGRAPH
Grant Halverson, www.granthalversonphotography.com

PHOTOGRAPH ON PAGES II – III
Woody with Rameses, the UNC mascot / PERSONAL COLLECTION

Library of Congress Cataloging-in-Publication Data

Durham, Woody.
  Woody Durham : a Tar Heel voice / by Woody Durham with Adam Lucas.
      p.   cm.
  Includes index.
  ISBN 978-0-89587-577-8 (alk. paper) — ISBN 978-0-89587-578-5 (ebook) 1.
Durham, Woody. 2. Sportscasters—North Carolina—Biography. 3. Radio broadcast-
ers—North Carolina—Biography. 4. North Carolina Tar Heels (Football team)—
History. 5. North Carolina Tar Heels (Basketball team)—History. I. Lucas, Adam,
1977- II. Title.
  GV742.42.D87A3 2012
  070.449796092—dc23
  [B]

                                                        2012020113

10 9 8 7 6 5 4 3 2 1

Design by Debra Long Hampton

To Jean, my wife and life partner for nearly 50 years and the mother of Wes and Taylor (who also became sports broadcasters) and the grandmother of Emily and Will, the best twins any grandparents could have

W. D.

To Stephanie, McKay, and Asher, who, in a household that is often consumed with buzzer-beaters, top plays, and scoreboards, constantly find new ways to remind me that life's true highlights happen away from the court

A. L.

Contents

Introduction | Walking through History   1

Chapter One | Beginnings   13

Chapter Two | The Undergrad Years   25

Chapter Three | Early Experience   37

Chapter Four | ACC Television   52

Chapter Five | Voice of the Tar Heels   62

Chapter Six | National Champions   75

Chapter Seven | From Heroes to Friends   87

Chapter Eight | World Travels   98

Chapter Nine | Chapel Hill   116

Chapter Ten | Outside the Booth   126

Chapter Eleven | The Family Business   137

Chapter Twelve | Transitions   150

Chapter Thirteen | Football Gets Close   167

Chapter Fourteen | Roy Williams Comes Home   177

Chapter Fifteen | NCAA Issues   189

Chapter Sixteen | Retirement   197

Acknowledgments   217

Appendix | Honored Tar Heel Players   223

Index   239

Opposite page: *In this publicity photo, Woody showed he had learned a few things from the high-flying scorers he covered.*
PERSONAL COLLECTION

Woody Durham
A Tar Heel Voice

Dean Smith surrounded by Woody and former players during the "Celebration of a Century"
event on February 12, 2010
COURTESY OF THE NEWS AND OBSERVER

Introduction

Walking through History

On February 12, 2010, I walked through history.

For several years before the University of North Carolina celebrated its 100th year of basketball, people would ask me, "How long are you going to do this job?" My response was that I was not sure how long I would continue to do radio play-by-play for the Tar Heels, but that I'd very much like to still be involved during the 100th season of basketball. After all, I was pretty sure I wouldn't be here for the 200th anniversary.

I knew the 100th season would be a big celebration of Carolina basketball. We had the NBA alumni game in September 2009, and that was a fantastic event. It was a great way to honor those players who were playing professionally and couldn't come back to Chapel Hill during the regular season because of their commitments to their teams.

Around that same time, Carolina announced it would be holding a "Celebration of a Century" the next February 12. At first, I'm not sure anyone knew what the event was going to be. Mostly, I was just hoping I would be asked to be involved. It wasn't an actual basketball game, so there wouldn't be a radio broadcast. There would be no play-by-play.

At the NBA alumni game, Carolina had brought in Ray Clay to do the public-address announcing because Michael Jordan was being honored and the university wanted fans to hear his famous "From North

Carolina . . ." introduction of Michael one more time. I wasn't sure what my role would be at the Celebration of a Century. Sometimes, other people emcee those big events. Stuart Scott has hosted the "Late Night with Roy Williams" festivities for many years and has done a wonderful job. I honestly thought Carolina might want to bring in a big personality to host the evening.

A committee was in charge of planning the event. I was not on the committee, but as February 12 got closer, Steve Kirschner, the associate athletic director for athletic communications, mentioned to me that I would be involved. What would I be doing? I had no idea.

The day before the event, we had a rehearsal on the floor of the Smith Center. That was the first time I knew anything about what was planned for the next night. That's also when I knew what a hit it was going to be. Members of the committee were there. They explained the "Centennial Fast Break," which would be the grand finale of the evening. It called for more than 20 players, all of whom had their jerseys in the Smith Center rafters, to pass the ball from one baseline to another, with me describing the action. At the end, Lennie Rosenbluth would pass the ball to Tyler Hansbrough, and Hansbrough would make a layup to complete the night. Later, Tyler would say it was the most pressure he had ever felt on a basketball court—over 20 legends passing him the basketball, 22,000 people watching him, and he had to make a layup or the whole thing was ruined. Can you imagine if he missed it?

Just as we finished the rehearsal, Roy Williams walked out on the Smith Center court with his wife, Wanda, his son, Scott, his daughter-in-law, Katie, and Scott and Katie's newborn son, Aiden. Coach Williams was carrying Aiden, and it was so obvious how proud of him he was. Things just felt right. Here were three generations of a family that had been so involved in Carolina basketball, and that's really what the night was supposed to be about—sons and fathers and grandfathers experiencing Carolina basketball together.

That's what I wanted to capture when I began writing the script for the opening segment of the evening. I thought about it when I was considering what to say. I found myself sitting and staring at the computer screen. I wanted something that wasn't the same old thing fans had heard from me before. This was a unique event. Based on what I knew about the night, I thought the fans would remember it forever. And if I was fortunate enough to be part of it, I wanted my contribution to be something they'd remember the same way.

Speaking in front of 22,000 people is a unique experience. These weren't just 22,000 strangers, though. These were 22,000 Carolina fans. We all had a shared background with the Tar Heels. I didn't have to explain to them why we loved it so much. But I did want to present it a little differently to them. I wanted to frame it in a way that maybe they hadn't thought about. That's why, standing out on the Smith Center court with the lights down, I started the evening this way:

"One hundred years of Carolina basketball."

That was almost all I had to say. People started cheering immediately. It was that kind of night.

"The Tar Heels got off to a late start with the basketball program. In 1911, Carolina was already 12 years behind Kansas, 10 years behind Syracuse, eight years behind Kentucky, and five years behind that school over on Methodist Flats in Durham."

I heard some booing then. They knew who I was talking about.

"But tonight, the Tar Heels are number two on the all-time victory list. One thousand nine hundred and ninety-seven wins. And they're number one in the average of most wins during a season, with 19.9 wins per season over the last 100 years. Four hundred and eighty-six lettermen and 18 head coaches have been responsible for it."

I went on to list the incredible numbers associated with the program and the players and coaches who had been part of it. It was an impressive list; it took nearly three full minutes to read all of it. Think about that: somewhere in the rafters was a banner for almost every one of those statistics. When you hear them so often, it can almost get routine. Carolina has been to 18 Final Fours, for example. Some schools build a statue for just one Final Four. When the 2009 national championship banner was unveiled at the pro alumni game, I had said over the PA, "Carolina is one of only three programs in the country to display at least six national championship banners." Around here, sometimes we get used to that level of success. The challenge is to explain it in such a way that makes people think, *Hey, that is pretty special.*

So at Celebration of a Century, I wanted everyone to understand that we weren't the best program because we started before everyone else. In fact, we started behind most of the other programs on that all-time victories list, yet we were ahead of everyone except Kentucky.

I like statistics like that. It's similar to Roy's winning percentage and the fact that he's the winningest active coach in the country. Sure, you can count the total number of wins, but the man has won 80 percent of his games, and that's the best figure in the country. So let other people say they have the most wins. There's nothing wrong with saying he's the winningest coach in the country by percentage. And if other people think that's sticking a little knife in there, well, maybe it is.

With regard to broadcasts, I've always said that I'm trying to talk to one person. It's the same thing even if you have 22,000 people sitting in front of you inside the Smith Center and you're talking to them over the PA microphone. If you talk to one person, everyone is going to understand you. That's what I tried to do that night. When you're out there on the court and the lights are down and you're standing in the spotlight, you're trying to work the entire arena. You want to get everyone in that building involved in the feeling of the night. At Celebration of a Century, that was easy. The fans were involved when they got out of their cars and walked in the door of the building.

Even with a crowd that big, I don't often get nervous about public speaking. That night, I was nervous. I had some nerves about the actual words I would say. But I was more nervous about keeping all the different segments going and making sure I was in the right place at the right time. The celebration had many different parts, including basketball and interviews and video. It had to be orchestrated just the right way. And after all that, do you know the only time I really had a problem? When I was interviewing Coach Williams on the side stage and he started to get emotional. Like most coaches, he is detail oriented. He had been very specific on the day of the event that he wanted it to run crisply and on schedule.

By the time I interviewed him, though, I think he saw what was happening. And he could feel it, too. Down on the court, you could almost feel the people buy in. At the start, they were a little unsure. But the committee had told me that when I finished my opening, I should turn toward the tunnel and say, "Here comes Carolina," and that would be the cue for all the alumni to run out onto the court. When I did that and I heard the crowd respond with a big roar, that's when I knew it was going to be a special night.

It made sense that Coach Williams would be emotional, because he puts his heart into Carolina basketball. For fans, Carolina basketball is something they love and want to be around. But to him, Carolina basketball is something he has lived for over three decades. We weren't just talking about basketball. We were talking about his life. He likes to say he is "corny as all get-out." I don't think it's corny. It's real emotion. During one of the interview segments, when I was sitting with him beyond one of the baselines and the crowd was listening via the PA, I could tell he was getting emotional.

It started when I asked him about the events of the weekend and all the alumni in town. "To me, it's a celebration of the greatest basketball program there is," Coach Williams said. "I feel very honored. I feel very flattered to be a very small part of the greatest program there is in college basketball."

I even said it right then: "We probably should quit right there." His eyes had welled up, and he was almost at the breaking point, and I thought, *Well, what am I going to do now?* I'm so glad he held it together until the end. But with 22,000 people roaring, I had to list the achievements he'd brought to the program since returning for the 2003–04 season. Six players whose jerseys were in the rafters. Three Final Fours. Two national championships.

I looked over at him and saw tears in his eyes. "You're a big part of what has gone on with Carolina basketball," I said. I'm glad we had a video coming up next because he was overcome with emotion. I tapped him on the knee and threw it to the video.

So much of that night was based on feel. At a normal game, television dictates almost everything that goes on. Television tells us when to take timeouts. It tells us how long halftime will be. As Coach Williams will tell you, because it's one of his pet peeves, sometimes it even delays the tipoff and keeps the players standing around. One year at Wake Forest, the players stood around for nearly two full minutes waiting on television to tell the game officials it was okay to start. Finally, Coach Williams pulled them all back to the bench. The referees knew what he was doing, but the crowd probably didn't. The players huddled around him, and he looked at them and smiled. "I don't have anything else to say," he said. "But we're not going to wait on them. They're going to have to wait on us." Just like he promised, he kept the players in that huddle until he was good and ready. By then, the television producers were fuming and wondering when the game was going to start.

At Celebration of a Century, we didn't have those restrictions. That meant we had time to stretch it out. At halftime of the alumni game, I interviewed Bobby Jones and Walter Davis at center court. They were in uniform—and looked like they could still play a pretty good game of basketball. We talked about Carolina's comeback from eight points down in 17 seconds on March 2, 1974. Davis hit a bank shot with no time on the clock to tie the score and force overtime before the Tar Heels eventually won.

I bet Walter has been asked about that play thousands of times since 1974, and he's probably met 50,000 people who claim they were in tiny Carmichael Auditorium that day. But he still smiled when he told the story. "Mitch threw me a great pass," Walter said. "I was trying to swish it, but it banked in."

"And what happened on Monday at practice?" I asked him.

"We went through the whole thing again, and Coach wanted to see if I could do it again," Davis said. "And I shot an airball."

As the crowd laughed, I felt like we had time for some ad lib. I sensed the crowd thinking, *I'd like to see Walter do that again.* And why not? That's when you have to listen to that feeling that's in the crowd.

"You want to try it again?" I asked him. We had never discussed this before, either during the audition or before the actual event. At that moment, it just seemed like the thing to do.

Someone rolled him a basketball, Walter took a couple dribbles, and his long jumper narrowly missed swishing through the rim. If he'd hit it, I think we could have all gone home. It might not have gotten any better than that.

To continue the theme from the 1970s, I interviewed Phil Ford next. We talked a little about the Four Corners offense and the role he played in making it so effective. Then I grabbed him by the arm and pulled him close to the sideline. "Come here a second," I told him. "We're probably going to need each other for what comes next."

That's when we played the Dean Smith video. Freddie Kiger, a great writer who has won Emmy Awards, had written it. It was a remarkable mix of happy memories of fun times on the basketball court, plus some sadness that those times were gone. We all knew the reality that Coach Smith was having some physical struggles. A lot of grown men were crying at that moment.

Maybe it was my age. I don't know if everyone was thinking the same thing as me. When I watched Coach Smith walk out of the tunnel with Roy Williams on one side of him and Bill Guthridge and Eddie Fogler on the other side, I wondered if we would ever see this again.

"A true legend is coming to center court," I said. And then I didn't say anything. The players were ringing the court, the lights were still down, and flashbulbs were popping everywhere. It looked like we were in the middle of a thunderstorm, thanks to all the flashes. Williams, Guthridge, and Fogler all moved off to the side and left Coach Smith in the middle of the center jump circle, and the crowd kept cheering.

The players came to him. Al Wood was the first one to hug him. It was exactly the right thing to do. At first, I wasn't sure if it was going to be a handshake or a hug, but a hug was exactly right. I remember looking at Al after they hugged, and he was wiping tears out of his eyes. I wondered if he was thinking the same thing as me: *will we ever get to do this again?* The guys who were on the inside of the circle—the ones closest to Coach Smith—were smiling and giving him a big hug. Once they backed up, I could see some tears.

What an emotional evening! How do you even try to follow that?

The grand finale was the Centennial Fast Break, and that's when I truly felt like I was walking through history. As the participating players went out on the court, the lights were down. The crowd members had no idea what they were going to see when the lights came back on. They could see people moving around on the court, but they didn't know, for example, that Tyler Hansbrough was standing next to Lennie Rosenbluth under one basket.

At the opposite basket, I was holding a basketball and standing next to Jim McCachren. "Ladies and gentlemen, we have something special for you to cap the evening," I said. "I don't recall this ever having been done in Carolina basketball history. Every one of these players standing on this court has their jersey in the rafters of the Smith Center."

Ninety-eight-year-old Jim McCachren, the oldest player in attendance, made the inbounds pass to Billy Cunningham. From there, 21 players touched the ball before Lennie passed it to Tyler. Every person in the Smith Center was standing. I could see in their faces how special it was for those players to be out there on the court. I was able to walk among them, going from player to player and saying something about each one of them. My only regret was that I had a written script in my hand. If I could do it again, I would love to find out who was going to be involved well beforehand and memorize what I said about them. Even up until the day of the event, though, we still weren't completely sure who was going to attend. Mitch Kupchak was originally scheduled to be part of the fast break, but his responsibilities with the Los Angeles Lakers prevented him from attending.

Anyone who understood anything about sports knew it was a unique moment. But for someone like me—someone who grew up going to games and following the Tar Heels—it was incredible. As I walked from player to player, I remember thinking, *I sure hope someone is getting a picture of this. When are Carolina basketball fans ever going to see something like this again?*

It was very much a full-circle feeling for me. There were people out there like Lennie, whom I had cheered for as a boy. And there were people like Mike O'Koren. He was someone my wife, Jean, and I had gotten to know before the NCAA had so many rules, when you could learn more about the players as people and spend time with them away from the basketball court. Jean has a barbecue chicken recipe that Mike loved, and he had been to our house for barbecue chicken. Mike even brought his girlfriend over to our house one time. He asked our sons, Wes and Taylor, who were 13 and six at the time, if they wanted to go out in the driveway and shoot baskets. Would they? Wes and Taylor were the only kids in Cary who went out and played basketball in the driveway with a Carolina All-American. Everyone knew who Mike O'Koren was.

Well, almost everyone. Mike's girlfriend went outside with them. Our neighbor was driving home about that time and saw her as he was pulling into the driveway. I noticed he nearly ran over the curb. Later, he asked me, "Who was that in your driveway?"

I said, "That was Mike O'Koren."

"Oh, was he out there, too?" he said.

"I could tell by the way you almost drove through the front yard that you had your eyes on other things," I told him.

That's how it was in those days. It was not highly unusual to get to know the players as people. Al Wood was another player we'd grown close to. Taylor was small at that time, but he would travel with us to some of the games. He'd always kid Al about his shooting and say, "Al, have you shot any more bricks lately?" Al would just laugh.

And here were Al and I, standing on a court 30 years later with some of the biggest names in Carolina history. Seventy players came back to play in the game, and many more than that were sitting in the stands watching their former teammates.

One of the players that night was Bill Harrison. He might have played fewer minutes than anyone who came back. He played basketball for one season and part of another, and then he went to Coach Smith and said, "Coach, I'm not contributing much to the team. I need to focus on my studies." Bill once told me that he wasn't sure how Coach Smith felt about him leaving the team, and he always wondered if he was upset about it. One night many years later, he went to eat at The Pines restaurant in Chapel Hill. Coach Smith was there, and they were able to talk. When Bill asked for the check, Coach Smith had taken care of it. That's when he knew for sure that Coach Smith wasn't upset with him. You're talking about the chief executive officer of JPMorgan Chase, one of the top five financial minds in the world. And he was out there running around with a T-shirt and shorts on because that's how much Carolina basketball meant to him.

As soon as I got home, Jean and I talked about how unbelievable it was to be part of the celebration. I don't recall a single hitch, and that was with only one rehearsal. There was so much love in that building. It wasn't just love from the fans to the players. It was love from the players to the program.

Being part of something that means so much to people is incredible. How lucky can you be? Over 40 years, Carolina basketball won 77 percent of the games I broadcast. Football won more than half the time. Put them together and Carolina won 72 percent of the time that I was on the radio. I'm not sure any other announcer in the country has been that fortunate.

When I was a kid, I would have liked to believe I would get to do something like that, but I didn't think it was really possible. Coach Frank McGuire and the 1957 basketball team were bigger than life to me, just like Charlie Justice and Art Weiner and those late-1940s football teams were bigger than life. And then it turned out that I would become friends with some of those individuals, and that on one night in February I walked among the best basketball players in Carolina history.

Think of all the places Carolina has taken me. I've seen 19,000 people in a sumo wrestling palace watching North Carolina play basketball. I've taken a bullet train from Tokyo. I saw every game Michael Jordan and Lawrence Taylor played for North Carolina. In 859 of Dean Smith's 1,133 games, I was able to talk to him before and after the game.

Looking at it on paper, I'm still not sure I believe it myself. People often ask me if being the voice of the Tar Heels was my dream job. Dream job? No. The job was beyond my wildest dreams.

Chapter 1

Beginnings

Maybe I was destined to be part of Chapel Hill. My mother's father, Taylor Fowler, was a barber on Franklin Street for many years. My father was basically raised in Chapel Hill. He was an avid sports fan, which made an early impression on me. Born in 1918, he was two years older than my mother. He remembered when Kenan Stadium was built. Growing up, he tried to go to as many football games as possible, and he had some creative ways of getting through the gates. Occasionally, he and his buddies would jump on the Coca-Cola truck when it was delivering drinks to the concession stands.

Neither of my parents went to college, which was typical for that time. They worked in the textile mills in Mebane. My mother was a winder. I remember stopping by the mill on the way home from school. She could come to the window and talk to me for a few minutes. My dad would later take some textile courses through the International Correspondence School, which was the equivalent in those days of taking courses online. But shortly after I was born on August 8, 1941, he was drafted into the army.

When he came back from the army, something important in my life happened: he bought North Carolina football season tickets. I didn't go to every single game, but I went to enough of them for it to be an important memory for me. The first years they had tickets were the Charlie Justice and Art Weiner teams of the late 1940s.

Coming from Mebane, we'd travel to Chapel Hill on Highway 54, a two-lane road. The traffic would be backed up for miles. The stadium held 27,000 people in those days. At that time, there was parking on Navy Field, and there was also an intramural field next to Woollen Gymnasium where we would try to squeeze our car. That was a typical football Saturday in Chapel Hill. No one thought about going to Franklin Street or which restaurant to hit after the game. No parking passes, no tailgating. It was about finding a spot to park, getting to the stadium, and watching the game.

Sometimes, I had a special reason for wanting to get to the stadium. I had an uncle who worked for Western Union. Telegrams were a big deal at that time. The Western Union office would get telegrams for Charlie Justice and some of the other players. My uncle knew where we sat in the stadium, and on several occasions he came by to get me, and I went down to the field house with him to deliver the telegrams. We'd go just inside the locker room door and usually deliver them to a manager, who would pass them on to the players.

But on a few occasions, we actually got to give them straight to Charlie Justice. Modern fans may not understand what an impact Charlie had on the game. He played nearly 70 years ago, and he still ranks fifth all-time at Carolina in both career total offense and career all-purpose yards. He's third all-time at Carolina in touchdowns scored and fourth in punting average. The entire town of Chapel Hill and much of the state of North Carolina were captivated by him. He wasn't big—just five-foot-nine, 165 pounds—but he could do everything. A popular song called "All the Way Choo Choo" was written about him. In a time when it was much more difficult for sports stars to be nationally famous, he was the hero of everyone who followed Tar Heel football.

Like almost everyone else in the area, I put him on a pedestal. Later, I stood in line at a Burlington department store for over an hour to get his autograph on a T-shirt. I once told him the story about waiting an hour for his autograph. "You didn't do that, did you?" he said. It was like he couldn't believe anyone would do that. And that's why those of us from that era were so impressed by him. Sure, he was a great football player. We're talking about someone who was such an icon that he was on the cover of *Life* magazine. But we never got the impression he was egotistical about his ability, or that being Charlie "Choo Choo" Justice had made him into a different person.

In second grade, five or six of my friends and I all got football uniforms for Christmas with Charlie's number 22 on them. The uniforms consisted of a jersey and a helmet with a chin strap underneath it. Home movie cameras were just emerging. One day, all of us wore our uniforms to school, and during recess one of the mothers came out to the playground and shot a movie of all of us. She developed it and showed it to us, and we thought we were the luckiest kids in the world.

We moved to Mount Holly in 1951 because my father took another job. Even after we left Mebane, we still came back to Chapel Hill to see relatives—at least that's why my dad said we came back. I think the real reason was to see football practice. We'd park on Raleigh Road, walk across what was then an intramural field, and cross Fetzer Field to watch the team practice on Navy Field.

Even after he graduated, I still kept an eye out for Charlie Justice. One season, he had trouble reaching an agreement with the Washington Redskins. He came back to Chapel Hill to work as a fundraiser for the UNC Medical Foundation and also helped out the football team as a volunteer coach. Larry Parker was a young player out of Charlotte who was being touted as the next Charlie Justice. Larry slowed up and ran out of bounds one day during a scrimmage. Charlie came running over to him, and you could hear his high-pitched voice all over the practice field: "Larry! Larry! Don't ever stop running! The worst I ever got hurt was when I slowed up going out of bounds and someone hit me."

Anything Charlie Justice said made a tremendous impression on me. You can bet I never slowed up and ran out of bounds.

When we weren't going to games or practices, we listened on the radio. My father thought Bill Stern, who did national games on NBC and then ABC Radio, was the best radio announcer he'd ever heard. On Saturday afternoons, we'd wash the car or be driving somewhere in the car, and we'd have the game on with Bill Stern behind the microphone. I'll never forget what my dad said about Stern: "He's really good. He almost makes you see it."

Often, when a team broke the huddle before an important play, Bill Stern would say, "What would you do? If you had to make this call, what would you do?"

Later, when we had an FM station in Asheboro that carried the Tobacco Sports Network, I listened to Ray Reeve and Bill Currie. My dad would always laugh at Bill's introductions of Ray because he called him "the squire of Wake County." Through the radio, they were our connection to the games. Ray used to do all 12 games of the old Dixie Classic— four games per day for three straight days. We think we have it tough today with four games a day for two days at the ACC Tournament. Ray did one more day, and he did the games all himself. I remember being impressed with his accuracy.

It wasn't until later that I began to know these radio personalities as people. There's an old story that Ray Reeve, a little under the weather due to some late nights on the town, insisted on doing a game against Miami at the Orange Bowl. He was firm in saying that he could do the game. So the crew hooked up a dead microphone and put it in front of him, and he did the entire game into a dead mic.

My dad was a sports fan, but he was also an athlete. All the mills had teams, and he played semipro baseball games on Saturday and Sunday. He was a pretty good third baseman. But my game was football. When we moved to Albemarle in 1953, I knew two things about the town. I knew it had been the 1940 champion in American Legion baseball, when it beat a team from San Diego that included John Ritchey, who was known as the Jackie Robinson of the Pacific Coast League. Over 10,000 people attended the final game of that five-game series. The other thing I knew about Albemarle was that the coach of the high-school football program was Toby Webb. His first year as head coach was 1947, and his reputation preceded him.

I played on the junior varsity in ninth grade and moved up to the varsity in 10th grade. I wasn't big—I weighed about 160 pounds—and wasn't very physical. As I told Coach Webb years later, "Coach, if I'd known about beer back then, I think I could have added some weight." My first year at Carolina, we'd go to Clarence's at night and eat a couple hot dogs and drink a couple beers. By the time I went home for spring break, I looked like someone had put an air hose up my rear end. I could have blocked some defensive ends at that weight.

In high school, I looked different. I had been a decent Little League baseball player, so I tried playing baseball my freshman season in high school. I could have really been a great player, except for one big problem: the pitchers started throwing curveballs. At that point, I decided I'd be better off talking about baseball than playing baseball.

In football, I started as a junior-varsity receiver and even caught a couple touchdown passes. We didn't have spring practice in those days, but we did have track practice. Basically, that was a glorified spring practice. Coach Webb took one look at me trying to be a running back in "track" practice and moved me to left guard. In 1957, when I was a junior, we finished 12–0 and won the Western North Carolina High School Activities championship. When we played Harding, the *Charlotte Observer* covered the game. The game was essentially over by halftime; we won 54–6. The next day, I read in the paper that the Harding players said we had on dark blue uniforms and played so well they thought they were playing against Duke. I know what you're thinking: that doesn't sound like much these days. But Duke was pretty good back then, so it was quite a compliment.

We played Lexington in what was called the Mud Bowl. It was Thanksgiving afternoon, and the game really lived up to its name. It had been delayed twice by rain. The field was a quagmire. Tommy Murrell was the starting left guard for that game, and he got hurt. I got the opportunity to play the rest of the game, which was a big deal. How much impact did I make? By the time we played Marion the next week for the

Woody with his high-school football coach, H. T. "Toby" Webb
PERSONAL COLLECTION

championship, the coach had put a substitute in that position.

I tried to contribute in other ways. As a senior, when I was an alternating starter and would often switch with a substitute on every play, I was sometimes the player Coach Webb used to carry in the plays. I've heard people ask Coach Webb what kind of player I was. His usual response is, "Well, he was awfully smart."

So I wasn't what you would call a great player, but being part of the team was so special. The entire town got caught up in Albemarle High School football. When we went on the road to play in places like Thomasville, Lexington, Kannapolis, and Concord, we would have as many or even more fans than the home team. That was partly because we were usually good, so we were the team to beat.

The Friday night of a home football game was a serious event. The stadium held about 6,000 fans. Big, permanent stands were on the home side and bleachers on the visitors' side. Coach Webb went to a coaching clinic in Greensboro one year and heard a lot of talk about the value of the pregame meal. From that point forward, we'd meet for a meal four hours before the game at a downtown restaurant. By the time we arrived at the stadium to get dressed, the place was already buzzing. There was an armory across the street from the school that hosted a pancake supper. When we came out for warmups, the stadium would be practically full. The first time Jean came to watch us play was against Charlotte Harding. She said when she walked into the stadium that night, she felt like the entire town was there. Everyone knew everyone, and they all looked at each other and said, "There she is, the girl from out of town."

When the game was over, it was just like you see in the movies. We'd go to a hamburger place, and all our teammates and friends would be there. There was so much camaraderie.

Coach Webb built most of that. I learned so much from him—not just football, but the way he handled people. He'd yell, but never at someone specific. He'd turn the game film on, and before we'd start going through it, he'd say, "Now, boys, anything I say right now doesn't mean anything personal." He was helping us get better. Given the choice, you'd rather have your daddy mad at you than Coach Webb mad at you.

He's been such an influential person in so many lives. He was more than a coach. He went on to become the principal at the junior high, then the principal of the high school, and finally the superintendent of the Albemarle schools. When his wife died several years ago, I went to see him with another former player, John David Moose. We were sitting on the deck of the Badin Inn & Golf Club, and Coach Webb said, "You know what? I kind of brought the school system through integration. You would not believe a lot of the phone calls I got in the middle of the night." We like to think of that as such a long time ago, but here was someone who was intimately involved in it, from whom we could still learn. Coach went on, "Nobody ever says, 'Toby, thank you for doing that for our school system.' All they want to talk about is what we did on the football field." He laughed about it, but it tells you how important football was to that community. Every Saturday morning I'm at home, I always check the Albemarle score in the paper.

Many of us count that as the formative time in our lives. John David Moose became an executive vice president with Collins & Aikman. Ed Crutchfield became president of First Union Bank at the age of 38. Wade and Roger Smith became two of the most important attorneys in the state. Bill Grigg became a chief executive at Duke Energy. His brother, David, became a prominent Albemarle attorney. Overall, our community raised plenty of successful lawyers, doctors, bankers, and other professionals. None of us would have been what we became without our hometown. We looked out for our own. Even Jean's father used to talk about it. "When you get around those boys from Albemarle," he'd say, "you can tell there is something different about them."

When I was 11 years old, my brother Dan was born. The day before I left for college, my youngest brother, Jim, was born. With such an age difference, it was difficult for us to have a close relationship.

Dan was almost from a different era because he came along in the 1960s, when America had changed drastically from when I grew up in the 1950s. He looked exactly like you'd expect a child of the 1960s and 1970s to look: he had the long hair, and we didn't see eye to eye on many things. But he was also a sports fan and a good athlete at Albemarle. He came to Carolina for a couple years and wanted to get into writing. Without telling anyone, he joined the navy. The recruiter told him, "We'll send you to journalism school at Indiana University." Well, by the time Dan was ready to go, journalism school was full, so the navy sent him to computer school in San Diego.

That was quite a change, but he made the most of it. He got his degree at the University of Washington and went to work in the Nordstrom computer department. I was on the West Coast with Carolina when he showed me his office. The computer center looked like the control room for a missile launch. Periodically, the screens would light up. He told me that every time a dot showed up on the screen, it was a cash register sale at a Nordstrom department store somewhere in America.

One thing you have to know about Dan: if he doesn't think something is being done the right way, he will tell you, and it doesn't matter if you are his boss, his wife, or his kids. So he's moved around some. He took his sons to watch a Carolina-Duke game at a sports bar in Seattle. On the ferry going back to Mercer Island, he had a stroke. He's slowly worked his way through some rehabilitation and is still living in Seattle.

My other brother, Jim, went into the air force. As his life progressed, I began to see that my brothers had a different home life with my parents from what I had experienced. I knew my parents drank socially. Almost everyone did. My dad loved the beach. Once a year, we would go to the beach for a week when the mill shut down. You never knew exactly which day it would be, but you knew that one day—it could be Tuesday, could be Wednesday, could be Thursday—my dad was going to get snockered. But at the time, I wouldn't have called that a problem. I don't even know if I would call it a problem now. He was from a generation that had lived through World War II. We didn't know the things he had seen.

Once I left home for college, though, I think the problems increased. They affected Dan's and Jim's childhoods more than they affected mine. At that time in America, if someone had an alcohol problem, they were sent to a state hospital like Dorothea Dix in Raleigh. It wasn't like there was a rehab facility where people went for those types of issues.

My dad had some depression that was caused by alcohol, and it caused him to lose his job. He tried some other careers but couldn't make anything work out. At that point, I didn't realize how deeply alcohol was affecting my mother, who also had other health issues.

One day, I got a call from a doctor friend, Dr. Freeman, who was in our church back home. He said, "Woody, your mom has been to see me for an exam. There's not much I can do for her. She has cervical cancer."

I went to see my parents without calling, which was something they were not expecting. When I got there, I was shocked at the state I found them in. They were really struggling. Not long after that, my dad died. He was 60 years old. They had started socializing with some families who had houses on Lake Tillery, and there were a lot of parties. When my father died, we were sitting in my parents' home in Albemarle. People from town came by. Out of the clear blue, one of the ladies with whom they socialized said, "Woody, I hope you don't think we caused this." I had never even mentioned the issue to her. That told me a lot about what had been happening. It was difficult for me. In some ways, I was far removed from the situation because I lived in Cary and then in Chapel Hill. But I was also the closest child to my parents because Dan and Jim were in other parts of the country and weren't very involved.

Having elderly parents, especially elderly parents with medical problems, is a major stress for everyone involved. It's a financial stress and an emotional stress. And with Dan and Jim gone, I had to figure out the best way to use what little money my parents had left to take care of them. That's a certain way to cause conflict in a family. Dan didn't like all the decisions I made, and I finally had to tell him, "Dan, you weren't there. I did the best I could." Jean was a tremendous help during that time.

After my dad died, my mom stayed in the house by herself. One weekend, I called her and she didn't answer the phone, though I knew she was there. We were living in Cary, and I decided to drive to Albemarle and see what was happening. I felt like I had walked into a scene out of a movie. It was exactly like people tell you it looks in an alcoholic's home. I found alcohol hidden everywhere, even in some ice buckets. At that point, the alcohol was more of a problem for my mother than her cancer.

My mother begged me not to put her in a hospital to get treatment for her alcohol problem. Eventually, with the help of some friends and an associate pastor from her church, she agreed to spend some time at the facility in Butner. I could check on her there. But I soon realized she also needed treatment for her cervical cancer. I brought her to the hospital in Chapel Hill because I knew how talented the staff was there. But it was too late. By then, the disease had spread so much.

I didn't think she would ever go home. Before she went into the hospital, we'd sold her house and set up an apartment for her. She wasn't drinking anymore, and she took immaculate care of that apartment. During my mother's final hospital stay, Jean and I moved everything out of her apartment and put it in a storage unit. Somewhat unexpectedly, she was then released from UNC Hospital. We had just moved to Chapel Hill at the time. When she was released, I drove her by our house. I wanted her to at least be able to see the outside, so she'd know where we were. I hoped we could move her somewhere close to us, so we could keep an eye on her. She wouldn't have it. She fought like hell until I agreed to move her back home.

Jean and I unpacked the storage unit to get her apartment ready. Ten days later, on Mother's Day weekend, she died.

I have never spent much time tracking my family tree. In some ways, I think that's because I was afraid of what I would find. For both of my parents, it was such an unfortunate ending. They didn't bear any similarity to the people I remembered from my childhood.

My brothers had a different experience at home, and that impacted the rest of their lives.

Jim did two tours of duty in the air force as a flight-line mechanic. When he left the armed forces, he worked for a private company building jets. He never had a good family life. I'll never forget one day that I talked to him on the phone. This was well after our parents died and near the end of his own life. I could tell he was drunk. I said, "Jim, are you okay?"

He said, "Woody, Daddy got me."

I knew what he was trying to say. He thought he was drunk because of our father. In the end, he couldn't handle that conflict and took his own life.

I don't feel it was fair to say, "Daddy got me." When I think about my childhood, I remember two loving parents who made me who I became. But what I have also come to realize is that, in a different way, my brothers believed our parents also made them who they became.

Memorable Moments

November 25, 1978 | Carolina 16, Duke 15

"Unbelievable, unreal! Famous Amos has taken it home."

Bob Holliday was working with me and doing the color, and Bob went crazy. Everybody thought it was me, but it wasn't. He went crazy. Carolina was down 15–3 late in the fourth quarter, and you know what happened—the aisles were full with people leaving. I would estimate the stadium may have been half full by the time of Carolina's final drive.

It was Dick Crum's first year as head coach, and with the Tar Heels down 15–10 he made the call for a draw play down on the goal line. If Amos Lawrence got stopped, the game was over because I think there was something like 11 seconds left, and Carolina had no more timeouts. So there was no way the team was going to be able to stop the clock. Maybe because the Tar Heels had thrown the ball so much in the last five minutes of the game, Duke was probably expecting them to try to throw to the end zone. Instead, they ran Amos on the draw play, and he scored a touchdown. It was wild. The players emptied the bench—I think they got a penalty for the celebration—right there in front of the old field house.

Chapter 2

The Undergrad Years

More than one person in our house is trained in the art of public speaking.
I met my future wife, Jean, at a summer debate workshop at Wake Forest.
It was the summer of 1957.

We didn't have a debate team in Albemarle. But I had done some
oratorical work, and a freshman English teacher named Mary Martin-
Hassell must have heard about it. She asked four students—Lane Brown,
Jo Parks, Pat Starnes, and me—if we wanted to go to Wake Forest for a
two-week debate workshop.

Jean was there representing Gray High School of Winston-Salem.
She already had debate experience, so she was good. The workshop was
run by a speech professor, Dr. Franklin Shirley. He later got into politics and became the mayor of Winston-Salem. Without fail, whenever
we encountered each other later in life, he would make a big joke about
how good Wake Forest had been to me—because that's where I met Jean.
I never did get onto the debate team, so it's a good thing I met Jean and
received something from the conference.

As we got to know each other, it turned out we actually had an unknown connection. Jean's neighbors across the street were the Eddins family, and Mildred Eddins's mother lived on Fourth Street in Albemarle. That gave us an easy way to see each other because Jean would come to Albemarle and stay with Mildred Eddins's mother. We dated for six years after meeting the summer before our junior year of high school.

When I returned home from the debate conference, the local radio station manager, Jake Presson, called to ask if I would come audition for him. At the time, I was trying to earn money working downtown in a shoe store. If I sold an orange box of shoes or a bright yellow box of shoes— those were usually the old-lady comfort shoes—I got a 50-cent bonus. That was not easy work, so I was excited about the opportunity to audition for Jake. He knew me because he had judged one of my oratorical projects.

Jake managed the second of two stations in Albemarle. For some reason, we just clicked. We were double-spotting, which meant we read two spots in a break. He would have one piece of copy in the control room, and I read the second spot if it was needed. Most businesses paying for sponsorships wanted to run their spots on Fridays and the weekends, so that's when the work was heaviest. When I made the decision to take that job, it meant I would have no time to debate, play football, work at the radio station, and still have any kind of social life.

It was imperative to reserve some time for a social life. Jean now says she didn't like me that much when she first met me, so I had some convincing to do. She thought I was a little arrogant because soon after we met I told someone, "I think she is going to be the one."

The debate conference ended on a Friday. Jean said, "What's going to come of this?" I told her I was going to call her, but I'm not sure she believed me. I called her the next morning. And for several weeks after that, I would drive the 68 miles to see her on Sundays. It was important to see her on Sundays. And why was that? Because on Sundays, she had time to cook, and she could really cook. The first time I went to see her, she made meat loaf, potatoes, green beans, and coleslaw. Both her parents worked, so she had grown up getting dinner started for her family. Soon after I met her, someone asked me about her, and I said, "She can really, really cook. I've got to go after her hard."

Woody and Jean's wedding photo - June 23, 1963
PERSONAL COLLECTION

Woody and Jean leaving on their honeymoon
PERSONAL COLLECTION

It wasn't always easy for us to stay in touch. In the late 1950s and early 1960s, distance was more daunting than it is today. In college, I went off to Carolina but Jean went to Meredith. Today, people think of those campuses as being almost side by side. It would be no big deal for two students to date.

In our era, we had two forms of communication: the post office and a telephone.

We wrote a lot of letters. In fact, I wrote Jean every day. It was four cents to mail a letter, and I'd say I got my money's worth. The week before we were married, she took every letter I had written her to her dad's house in Winston-Salem. She went through the entire box, read them all, and saved three. I guess I must not have been much of a writer.

When we wanted to talk on the telephone, it wasn't as simple as just calling her number. We had to make person-to-person calls. She had a phone in the hall of her dorm at Meredith. I'd make a person-to-person call, which meant it was operator assisted. I wasn't charged unless Jean was available. I became an expert in placing person-to-person calls.

That was probably the toughest time in the 54 years we've known each other, including the 49 years we've been married. We physically saw each other roughly every six weeks. Other than that, it was all letters and phone calls. Today, if you go six weeks without seeing someone, they might as well disappear from the planet.

I didn't have access to a car during my freshman year at Carolina. Although it made me nervous to borrow my grandfather's car, I would sometimes take it to pick her up. He'd let us use the car all weekend. If it was a really big weekend—a special occasion—we'd go to the Ranch House for the Sunday buffet. It was owned by the same family that owned the Rathskeller on Franklin Street, and it was fine dining. In fact, it was so good that in 1963 its New Year's Eve dinner, which included steak and champagne, cost $5.50 per person. In college, I could sometimes make $5.00 stretch for several days, so that was serious money. I would cash a $5.00 check at Y Court, and that would last for two or three days. Jean was living on a budget of $10.00 per week.

Cashing a check at Y Court was a real pleasure for me because I found out the cashier, Mary Maultsby, had a son who was coaching football in Albemarle. That meant she made a lot of weekend trips there. I'd tag along, usually with two or three other friends. That was how you were able to go home: you found a friend of a friend who had a connection, and everyone rode together.

Since Jean and I couldn't always talk on the phone or write letters, we had to be creative about how we communicated. At that time, Jimmy Capps was on WPTF, the local radio station. At 11 P.M., he had a show called *Our Best to You*, during which he would play requests. From what I heard, it was a popular show in the dorms at Meredith. All the girls would stay up to see if they got a dedication. You'd hear Jimmy Capps say things like, "This one goes out to so-and-so on the third floor at Peace from Ronald on the third floor at N.C. State." It was a really big deal on college campuses.

Our song was "Personal Possession" by Nat King Cole. I still remember the lyrics:

> You're my personal possession,
> That's what you are.
> You're my magnificent obsession,
> My lucky star.

Nat King Cole might have been a little better writer than me. Jean might even have kept all the letters if he had been my ghostwriter.

Eventually, Jimmy Capps moved over to WKIX. I had the opportunity to meet him years later, and I was shocked. I had always pictured the big man who possessed that booming voice. But he was just a little bitty guy. I had to keep from laughing when I shook his hand because I couldn't believe the voice I'd listened to for so many nights came out of that person.

In high school, it was unusual to date someone from outside Albemarle. By the time we got to college, it was more common, since college brought us together with a whole different group of people. That sometimes meant we had to be creative with the hometown girls. Wade Smith had graduated three years earlier than I from Albemarle High and went on to play football at Carolina. In college, though, no one knew that one day he would be one of the biggest lawyers in the state of North Carolina. One day, he got a call from a girl who had been his steady in high school and whose mother owned a children's dress shop in Albemarle. This girl was about to make her debut at the Raleigh debutante ball, which as you can imagine was a big deal. She wanted Wade to escort her.

"I can't do it. I have football practice," he told her.

The next day, he had a note in his locker from the head football coach, Jim Tatum. He went to see Coach Tatum.

"Wade," the coach told him, "I got a phone call from Albemarle this morning."

Wade got nervous. "Coach, I've already talked to her," he said. "She knows I can't do it."

Whatever had been said in that call made a big impression on Coach Tatum. "Wade, this is the kind of thing I want our players to do," he said.

Imagine that happening today. I doubt T. J. Yates went to too many debutante balls during the season.

Wade tried to get out of it by saying he didn't have a car, but Coach Tatum was ready for that one. "I just picked up my new dealer car yesterday, and you can use that," he said.

Wade's last try would have made sense to almost any football coach: "Coach, I'd have to miss practice."

But for some reason, Coach Tatum didn't mind. So, for several days at 3 P.M., Coach Tatum would grab a bullhorn and announce, "Wade, it's time for you to go to Raleigh!"

You can just imagine the flak the future top attorney in North Carolina took as he left Navy Field and went walking through the woods to the old field house. In hindsight, it makes person-to-person calls and daily letters seem like a small price to pay.

Because Jean was not in Chapel Hill with me, I had to adjust socially to college life on my own. My first roommate was Fred Croom, a Morehead scholar from Maxton, North Carolina. Of course, having a Morehead recipient in my Stacy Dorm room made me constantly think about how

I had kicked the interview in the regional round. I was amazed at how much Fred could get out of a book in a short amount of time. His dad was a doctor, and Fred just had the knack for doing well in school. He majored in chemistry and went on to become a chemistry professor at the University of Tennessee and later the provost at the University of the South.

My sophomore year, Fred moved into a fraternity, and I initially went back to Stacy. Because the university was so crowded, I was in a three-man room. It didn't take long before I moved out of there and into Parker Dorm with Frank Crowell. Talk about a small world: Frank was from Nashville and would later do the PA for Vanderbilt basketball games. In later years, I roomed with Drew Grice as a junior and Ken Mayhew as a senior.

The campus we knew was different from the one students see today. On Franklin Street, there was a series of nice clothing stores—Milton's and Town & Campus, plus Robbins Department Store. We had two movie theaters—the Carolina and the Varsity. What was the main courthouse also includes a post office. Across from the post office was Kemp's, a record place that had every album you could ever want. For books, we always went to The Intimate, which was owned by Wallace Kuralt, the brother of Charles Kuralt.

As you walked up Franklin past The Intimate, you came to a young men's clothing store where Spanky's is now located and Huggins Hardware where Starbucks is today. The hardware store was owned by Vic Huggins's family. Vic was most famous for being the Carolina cheerleader who came up with the idea of the ram mascot. He spent $25 to buy a ram from Texas. It debuted in 1924. The ram was in honor of a running back named Jack Merritt, who was known as "the Battering Ram." But the idea might have taken hold because of a kicker. The new ram was on the sidelines during the game against Virginia Military Institute on November 8, 1924. A kicker named Bunn Hackney rubbed the ram's head before he attempted the eventual game-winning field goal, and the ram was here to stay. If Bunn Hackney had missed that kick, people might be cheering for a different mascot today.

Carolina fans know that the ram mascot is always at football games but never at basketball games. I once asked Vic Huggins why he didn't bring the ram to basketball games.

"Oh, we tried," he told me. "But he pooped on the floor at the Tin Can."

That's a good reason for why fans don't see the live ram at the Smith Center.

A couple of famous Franklin Street restaurants that multiple generations of Carolina graduates will immediately recognize were the Zoom Zoom and the Rat. In those days, we had to save up for a couple days before we could go to the Rat and get a Double Gambler.

Traveling to and from town was completely different from the way it is today. Going toward Durham, the only thing on the two-lane road was WCHL in a white cinder-block building. Going the other way, toward Raleigh on Highway 54, once you got past Glen Lennox—where a dairy bar was located—there was absolutely nothing. Chapel Hill has seen significant changes. Some people might think the changes are for the better, while some might say they are for the worse. But it feels like the area has changed with what the times have demanded.

In my studies, one of my most fortunate strokes of luck was getting into Dr. James Harland's archaeology class. He was an extremely popular professor, to the point that students would try to buy class tickets to get into his course. Part of his popularity was due to his personality. My first day of class, he stepped up on a raised platform to show slides, and the pointer he was using was a golf driver with the head taken off. A story was told that the student who created the pointer for him had received an A in the class in exchange.

It was unheard of to get a C in his class, because if you showed up on all the class days you would get an A. But I had a friend, Doug Squillario, who got a C in Dr. Harland's class. Doug went to see Dr. Harland and said, "I really need to make a B in order to get into law school." Of course, Doug had no intention of going to law school. I wouldn't be surprised if Dr. Harland knew that, too. But he was such a compassionate man that he picked up the class roll book, erased the C, and replaced it with a B.

I made two mistakes with my class selections.

My junior year, I went to see Boss Wynn, who was the head of the radio and television department. "Boss," I told him, "I think I want to take Econ 43."

Boss Wynn had a voice that sounded like God talking. "Oh, no," he said. "You don't want to do that. People have a lot of trouble with that class. Take Econ 31."

But I knew that if I took Econ 31, I also had to pass Econ 32 in order to get any credit.

"It's okay," he told me. "You won't have any trouble with it."

You know what happened next: I flunked Econ 31. I knew I was in trouble on the first day of class because the professor was German. I'd had him for math my freshman year and had trouble understanding him. But I also had a philosophy that reminds me a little of what Roy Williams tells his players when he doesn't call a timeout when they feel they might need one: "You got yourself into trouble. You get yourself out of trouble." So I didn't go to drop-add to get out of the course, and I ended up having to retake it in summer school.

The only other course that troubled me was psychology. I never re-took that one. I decided I'd met Pavlov's dog enough times already.

Carolina sports were not particularly successful when I was an undergraduate. Football was going through the Jim Hickey years, and some young assistant named Dean Smith had just taken over the basketball team. I did some baseball on the radio and was paid five dollars per game. Some of the old-timers talk about the days when Ted Williams was on campus for his navy preflight training, and how he hit the longest ball they ever saw when he bounced one off the side of Lenoir Hall. Well, Ken Willard hit the longest ball I've ever seen during one of those games I did on the radio. That thing was still going up when it went over the left-center field fence. The last I saw of it was when it scraped through the tops of the pine trees.

Despite the lack of on-field success, athletics were still a big deal. One year, I had a biology class near Kenan Stadium on Saturday morning. Each day we had a home game, I'd go to class dressed in a shirt, a tie, and a jacket because that's what we wore for home games. It was like a fashion show for the women, particularly the ones from out of town. Jean tells me that Thursday nights at Meredith were like a fashion runway. The ladies would lay out what they planned to wear to Saturday's games at whatever schools their dates attended. We really put some thought into what we were going to wear. If you look back at the pictures from that era, you'll see an all-necktie crowd. Don't worry, though: the outfits didn't keep anyone from having a little bit of fun, and maybe even a little bit to drink.

Carolina had instituted an alphabetical ticketing system during the frenzy of the 1956–57 basketball season. For example, for the first game, students with last names beginning with the letters *A* through *M* had first priority on tickets. For the second game, it would be *N* through *Z*. By the time I was an undergrad, you could usually get tickets no matter what. It might not be as good a seat as you wanted, but you'd at least have a ticket.

It was a big deal to see the athletes around campus. Larry Brown always looked like he just stepped out of *GQ*. What I later found out was that the basketball team almost underwent some major changes when Dean Smith replaced Frank McGuire. Several players on that first Smith team have said they considered not coming back to school. They knew what kind of work he was going to require because Coach McGuire had often left Coach Smith in charge when he was away recruiting. Eventually, they decided to give Coach Smith a chance, but it wasn't an easy decision for them.

Memorable Moments

January 17, 1979 | Carolina 70, N.C. State 69

"Austin coming frontcourt, across the timeline with 10 . . . Knocked away, Dudley Bradley! Dudley Bradley for the stuff! Seventy to 69, three . . . two . . . one . . . Matthews off-balance, off the glass. Dudley Bradley's defense did it!"

It did: Dudley Bradley's defense did it. A lot of people forget the Tar Heels were up by 21 at the half, 40–19, and N.C. State came back and took the lead. Dudley had taken the ball away from Clyde Austin earlier in the game, so that's why Austin was so conscious of where he was on the court. He saw Bradley coming and wanted to change direction and get away from him.

Caulton Tudor, the *News & Observer* columnist, has a funny story about the aftermath of the game. Someone asked Austin what happened. He said, "I was going frontcourt with the ball. I saw Dudley and tried to move away from him, and the next thing I know, Coach is calling me a sonofabitch."

At Reynolds Coliseum, we did the games from way up in the rafters. When Dudley made the play, I thought Bob Holliday was going to fall out of our broadcast position. On the tape of the play, though, you hear only my voice because we recorded my audio straight onto the videotape the coaches used for the game film, and Bob's microphone was a separate line.

Chapter 3

Early Experience

Being involved with oratory had two major benefits for me: it indirectly led me to meet Jean, and it created an opportunity for my first job in radio. My father was in the Optimist Club, and his club had an oratorical contest for middle-schoolers. To enter, I had to write a five-minute presentation and then deliver it from memory. I was fortunate to win the local contest three times. The winners of the local contest moved on to the Optimist State Convention.

The first time, I won third place, which meant I got a trophy. In my second appearance, I won second place. In my final entry, I thought I had won third place. After the contest ended, I went back to Albemarle with the third-place trophy. One day, I received a call from Dr. Carl Bowen, an Albemarle dentist who later became president of Optimist International. He had been helpful in preparing me for the contest. I had stood behind a high-backed chair in his living room to simulate a podium, and he critiqued my speech as I gave it. When he called, he said, "Woody, we had a miscount of the votes in the oratorical contest. You actually tied for second." I was presented with a second-place trophy at a later Optimist meeting. So in my last oratorical contest, I won two trophies.

That wasn't the most important outcome, though. Jake Presson was a local judge in several of the contests. Jake managed one of the radio stations in Albemarle and was looking for a student announcer. My part-time job at Merritt Shoes had taught me an important lesson: I never wanted to work in retail. At that point in my life, I'd found more things I didn't want to do than I did want to do. I'd also had a job delivering papers, and I got a job washing cars from a coworker of my father at the mill who bought a service station. The station had two employees who washed cars: the son of the owner and me.

I also did some PA work at high-school basketball games. I did PA during one of our high-school games that took place at the same time Carolina and Duke were playing. Of course, I was keeping up with the Carolina-Duke game. I thought everyone else might want to know the score, too. Periodically, I gave score updates. The basketball coach, Ken Frasier, was fine with that when I did it during the timeouts. One time, I got a little carried away and gave the score as someone was preparing to go to the free throw line in our game. Coach Frasier made it clear he didn't need any more Carolina-Duke scores during his game.

So when Jake Presson asked me to come by the station, I had some work experience. It was a summer Friday afternoon. In those days, most of the commercials were read, rather than recorded. The announcer would play a record, then read a spot. When he read two spots back to back, it was called double-spotting. Three spots in a row was triple-spotting.

The audition was simple. Jake read the first spot of a double spot, then cued me to read the second spot. I had been around a radio station before, since two of my good friends worked at Albemarle's other radio station. But I'd never read anything in the studio. The first spot I had to read was for Veteran's Grill, which was on the highway between Albemarle and Salisbury at a little crossroads called Gold Hill. It was a service station where people could also get sandwiches. When I went back into the control room after reading the spot, Jake said, "You seemed really comfortable there."

He offered me the job, which was for assignments on the weekend. I took it with the understanding that I would still play football. He also asked if I could come into the station and work an hour before school. Jake's radio show started at 8 A.M., so my job was to sign the station onto the air and start the music. By the time I got to school, I had already worked an hour.

Soon, we worked out a deal with Mr. Paul Fry, the mixed chorus teacher, who would let me out of school 10 minutes early. I had an old gray Plymouth that my dad had gotten for my junior and senior years of high school. I'd leave school and drive to the station. When my friends got out of school at 3:00 P.M., they'd turn on the radio. By the time the news was over, around 3:05 or 3:10, I'd be playing rock-and-roll records on the radio.

I was the youngest employee at the station, which meant I got all the jobs no one else wanted. I did the dirty work. I was there early in the morning when no one wanted to be. But the job also gave me an incredible amount of experience in a variety of situations. The most unique by far was the church remotes.

To do a church remote, I'd set up a couple of microphones on Sunday. Our competing station, WABZ, did a different church every Sunday. At WZKY, we did a church for a longer period of time—usually a month's worth of services—before we switched to another church. In my first week doing the remote from the First Christian Church, we had line trouble, as I could hear on my headset after a few minutes. I had a ballpoint pen, so I grabbed a church bulletin and wrote, "Line trouble!" on it and tried to show it to the preacher while he was starting his sermon. I guess I thought he would pause the service while our radio station solved the technical difficulties. In today's sports television world, the game would probably be stopped for technical problems like that.

Sometimes, the station would send me to a church where I'd never been before. At the Church of God, the Reverend Delk was the minister. He had a son and daughter who were in school with me, but I'd never been to church there. His church did what was called "the birthday song." It had a jazzed-up piano and a lady who could really play it. When she played the birthday song, the idea was that anyone who had a birthday that week would come down and put an offering in the plate. One Sunday when I was doing my remote, she played her jazzed-up piano, but nobody came down the aisle. The song ended. Reverend Delk went to his pulpit, stood as tall as he could, and looked down at the congregation. "Well, brothers and sisters," he said, "the response was not very good, so we are going to sing another verse of the birthday song." Some people must have suddenly remembered their birthdays, because when the congregation sang the second verse a procession of people came down the aisle to make a contribution.

Ol' Woody was ready to get out of there as soon as noon came and we went off the air. At the end of the service, members of the congregation at the front of the church fell down on their hands and knees, recommitting themselves. Well, they were in my way. As they fell all over the place, I had to crawl over them, trying to wrap up my cords and collect my microphones.

In addition to the church remotes, my job gave me my first opportunity at broadcasting sporting events on the radio. Since I worked at a daytime station, we'd do a Tuesday-night basketball game and play it back on Wednesday afternoon when school was over. As you'd imagine, it was a pretty big deal to get out of school and hear your name on the radio scoring a basket or getting a big win. We'd also do a Friday-night game and play it back on Saturday morning.

I did the color, and a man named Nealson Russell did play-by-play. He'd come to our station from WABZ. He was a big, heavyset guy whom everyone called "Fat Boy." In fact, that was the name of his radio show at the old station. He was an old-fashioned homegrown announcer. He really put a local spin on things. For high-school home games, the "press box" was the library. It was on the third floor, and we could see everything from there. Nealson once called a field goal by Larry Mullis this way: "Larry really got a toe into that one. He kicked it clear over the street into Mr. Jones's yard." Someone named Mr. Jones actually did live near the school, but only Nealson would have described the kick that way.

I really enjoyed the sports aspect of my job. The combination of my dad's rabid fandom and being involved with the Albemarle football program had ingrained in me a deep love of sports. It was so important in the community that it got into my blood.

I loved all sports. One summer, I sold and broadcast Little League baseball games. We went on the air at 5 P.M. and had to do a six-inning baseball game before we went off at sundown. Selling was easy. I knew that some of the parents of the players had oil companies and hardware stores, so I'd ask them for sponsorships. I could make $50 here and $50 there and end up with a little bit of a commission. Don't laugh at Little League baseball—I supplemented my radio Little League money with newspaper Little League money. The *Stanly News and Press* paid me $10 a week to write Little League columns. I kept track of scores, batting averages, that week's home runs, and anything that could get more names into the paper.

Being involved with the radio station was a positive from the very beginning. When our family went on vacation for a week, I missed my work. We'd come back into town on Sunday, and I'd usually be over at the station by the end of the day. While we were gone, I thought about how I could do a better job with specific details, and I wanted to put them into action as quickly as possible.

Jake Presson was a tremendous mentor. He even advised me to go to the summer high-school radio-television institute at Carolina. It was like basketball camp, except it was for radio and TV. It was led by the same college professors who taught radio and television classes at Carolina. It enabled me to get familiar with them and with Swain Hall and the studio for WUNC-FM.

When I first started at WZKY, it was a big deal. I'd run into people who would be excited and say, "I heard you on the radio!" The longer I was there, the more I was accepted. I stayed with the station until the summer between my junior and senior years at Carolina, when I got the opportunity to do some Carolina baseball games on WCHL—for the big price of five dollars per game. It wasn't like I was the Wolfman Jack of Albemarle, but it was a tremendous experience.

At Carolina, with a few exceptions, my experience started to shift to television. My first semester, I didn't do much other than go to class and try to learn my way around Chapel Hill. But in my second semester, I began to stop by the Channel 4 offices. At that time, the station's sports reporter was Don McCarson. He had been the minister of music at Jean's church in Winston-Salem. At the end of my sophomore year, he left to take another job. As soon as my junior year began, the station asked if I was interested in his spot. That was my first opportunity to be on camera.

For me, it was like being in a lab every day. You go to school to get an education. There are times when that education is as much out of the classroom as inside the classroom. That's not to say that I didn't have some terrific professors, because I did. I was fascinated by a religion course with Dr. Boyd. I was so enthralled with listening to him that sometimes I didn't do as much note taking as I should have. William Geer in political science was a wonderful lecturer. I also had George Taylor in political science. His was such a popular class he had to do it in the big auditorium in Carroll Hall. In fact, Dr. Taylor later hosted a half-hour television show on Channel 4, so I was able to get to know him outside the classroom. By that point, a great deal of my education was coming in some form or fashion in those Channel 4 offices.

I started with the midday news because I had a class break at that time. I also did the 6 P.M. sports strip and the Saturday football games. It was an incredible amount of practical experience, and I made the effort to learn more than just the on-camera jobs. I didn't learn the intricate details of how a camera works, but I made sure to know what a director did and how a producer organized a broadcast.

Working at Channel 4 also gave me my first contact with an assistant basketball coach named Dean Smith. We did Broadvision broadcasts of the basketball games, which meant we televised the video, and viewers would watch it on their televisions while listening to the audio on their radios. It was the forerunner of the "turn down the sound" movement that became popular many years later.

When Carolina had a home basketball game, I did my sports spot on the 6 P.M. news from Woollen Gym. Usually, the station asked me to have Frank McGuire on as a guest. I believe he may have done it once, but usually he sent his assistant, Dean Smith. The basketball offices were right around the corner from our broadcast location, so in those days—it would be very different today—it was no problem to get a coach to stop by.

At that point, I knew nothing about Coach Smith's background except for his time at the Air Force Academy. It's hard to think of him this way now, but he just wasn't a big deal. He was a Carolina assistant coach. That was the extent of everything most people knew about him. My best initial impression of him was when he showed up for our first interview and took the time to learn all the names of the crew involved with the broadcast. And when he came back for his second interview, he called everyone by name. That's the first time I realized how sharp he was.

Assistant coaches were much more low-profile at the time. In fact, Carolina basketball in general was much more low-profile. Even though Frank McGuire had coached the Tar Heels to the 1957 national championship, the basketball offices were tiny. There was a rumor that the football coach, Jim Tatum, had decided to expand the football offices while McGuire was on a recruiting trip. When McGuire came back from New York City, all his furniture was in the hall.

The basketball offices were down by the men's room. When you went to visit a coach, the first thing you came to was the secretary's desk. The place was so small you had to turn sideways to slide between the secretary's desk and the wall. I can honestly say a lot of things have changed.

I was home in Albemarle in the summer of 1961 when Coach McGuire left for the Philadelphia Warriors. When it was announced that Dean Smith would be the new head coach, many fans said, "This guy is from where? He coached at the Air Force Academy? What have we done?" The common perception was that Carolina, only four years removed from an undefeated national championship, was now de-emphasizing basketball.

Many years later, I had a conversation with Chancellor Aycock, the man who had to decide how to replace McGuire. He told me that Coach McGuire came to his office to tell him he was leaving. The chancellor said, "Is it all right if I talk to Coach Smith?"

Coach McGuire responded, "Sure, he's out in the car."

The chancellor brought him into the office and less than 10 minutes later hired him as the new basketball coach. They were familiar with each other from Coach Smith's work with the research into the NCAA problems over recruiting violations. The chancellor had to go to San Francisco to meet with the NCAA committee, and Coach Smith had gone with him. More than anything he had done on the basketball court, it was the thoroughness of his commitment to his NCAA work that had impressed Chancellor Aycock.

Being involved with Channel 4 provided me valuable practical experience. It was also a place to make connections. By the time I graduated in 1963, I felt good about the amount of experience I had. I didn't believe many recent college graduates out there had put in as much work as I had.

At the end of my senior year, I auditioned for WIS in Columbia, South Carolina. That station was looking for a full-time sports guy. It was a significant opening because the University of South Carolina was in Columbia and Frank McGuire was there as the basketball coach. The general manager, Charles Batson, took me to lunch at the City Club. The station had some misgivings because I was seen as someone who had done "educational television." The people there weren't sure if I could do commercials. The staff at Channel 4 helped me put together some demo tapes to try and prove I could do what I'd have to do at WIS. Of course, I also had some misgivings about WIS. I didn't know if I'd be able to refer to South Carolina as "Carolina," as the people in that area—and only that area—do.

At the same time I was talking with Columbia, I had another opportunity. As part of Wes Wallace's journalism class, students took a two-day trip to Charlotte, where we were exposed to WBT and WBTV. Those connections created an opportunity for me when I received a call from Bill Melson, the personnel director for Jefferson Standard Broadcasting. He told me about an opening at a television station in Florence, South Carolina. On a staff of four broadcasters, one had just left. "It's not a sports job," Bill told me, "but I think it would be good for you to get some commercial television experience."

I drove to Florence. I met the program director, George Burnett, and did an audition, and he hired me on the spot. Less than a week after I got back, WIS called and made me an offer. I had to say I had already accepted a job in Florence. The offer in Columbia would have been great—it was a full-time sports job—but I think it was someone's way of telling me that I wasn't meant to refer to the University of South Carolina as "Carolina."

Just like my early days in radio, I was the young guy on the staff in Florence. Dave Rogers, who was the voice of NASCAR's Southern 500, did the studio sports at 6 P.M. and 11 P.M. for the station. I was the early-morning guy and also did the kids' show. The station's weatherman, Ashby Ward, had just moved into the news anchor position. Carolina Power & Light sponsored the weather, and if you did the weather, it meant an extra $5 a night. The station had an audition between Joe Nicholson, who had been the substitute weather guy, and me. I felt really good about my audition, and would have felt even better about the extra $25 a week. But in the end, CP&L's advertising agency selected Joe. I was disappointed. It wasn't that I thought I had a future being a weatherman, but it was a competition, and I wanted to win it.

Shortly thereafter, I got a phone call from WFMY in Greensboro. I had been in Florence only four months, and if I'd gotten that weather spot, my reaction to WFMY might have been different. By the end of October, I was back in Greensboro with WFMY. If I'd stayed in Florence, it's very possible that my career path would have been different. It's amazing how something you think is a negative at the time can turn into a tremendous positive.

I started at WFMY on November 1, 1963. Three weeks later, President Kennedy was shot. I played golf at Tanglewood that day. Jean was teaching school then, and when I got back to our apartment she met me in the parking lot. She was emotional.

"What's the matter?" I asked her.

"The president has been shot," she told me.

There was still a 6 P.M. newscast to do, and I knew I had to get to the station immediately. I changed clothes and went to WFMY. By the time I got there, I learned the president was dead. Carolina-Duke football was going to be the ACC game of the week that Saturday. That evening, it was postponed to Thanksgiving Day. That entire weekend happened in slow motion.

WFMY was generous in allowing me to do a variety of other jobs while I was with the station. I worked on the Wake Forest network doing color beginning in 1964. But when the university changed head coaches, I decided to leave the broadcast. Not long after that, Herb Appenzeller, the athletic director at Guilford College, called me with a proposition. We had become friends because WFMY gave Guilford good coverage. "Don't laugh at me," Herb said. "I want to know if there's any way you would consider doing our games at Guilford. We can't pay you much."

What he didn't know was that he was offering me as much as Wake Forest had paid to be on its broadcasts. I did Guilford games for two years. It was fun to keep my hand in football and to see that small-college side of the game that we miss sometimes today. At the same time, I missed the atmosphere of big-time college football.

I maintained my connection with the daily happenings of big-time college sports through my relationship with the ACC Network, established by C. D. Chesley. Most of what we know and love about ACC basketball on television today can be traced back to Ches. I got an early taste of being involved with that network through my work at Channel 4. Soon after that, I decided my long-term goal was to be the play-by-play man for ACC basketball and football games. If you had asked the Woody Durham who was a student at Carolina where he wanted to be in 10 years, I would not have said doing the radio broadcasts for the Tar Heels. I would have said doing the ACC game-of-the-week broadcasts in basketball and football.

What I didn't know was that I would soon get a chance to be part of those games. And just like some of my previous career moves, it was not always the part I wanted that would lead me to my destination—back to Chapel Hill.

Woody's sportscasts at WFMY-2 in Greensboro were award-winning.
PERSONAL COLLECTION

Woody interviewing golf legend Arnold Palmer
PERSONAL COLLECTION

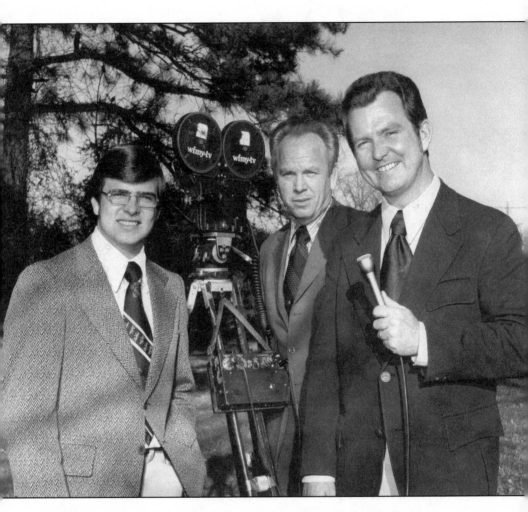

Sports reporter Johnny Phelps, sports photographer Grady Allred, and Woody—the WFMY-2 sports crew
PERSONAL COLLECTION

Woody filing a television report from the Charlotte Motor Speedway

Memorable Moments

September 12, 1981 | Carolina 56, East Carolina 0

"Give to Bryant. Bryant, 30, 25, 20, steps out of a tackle and he's going again. Touchdown Kelvin Bryant, number five as the Tarboro junior goes 33 yards. And he's taking the ball to Steve Streater! He gave the ball to Steve Streater in the end zone!"

That was one of the most emotional games I ever had at Kenan Stadium. I could feel it in the crowd. It was East Carolina, and it was a full house. When Kelvin Bryant already had four touchdowns, the team was huddled near the 50-yard line. And he stood up in the huddle and pointed at Steve Streater, who was in a wheelchair down near the end zone. Steve had signed with the Redskins, then come back to Chapel Hill and had a car accident on a slick highway leaving the airport. The accident paralyzed him.

When Kelvin scored, he put the ball in Streater's lap, and Steve spiked the ball.

I went to a dinner with Coach Dick Crum in Tarboro honoring Kelvin, and Coach Crum said, "There wasn't a dry eye in the house." I agree with that.

Chapter 4

ACC Television

My first opportunity to do Atlantic Coast Conference games on television came when I was still an undergraduate. C. D. Chesley occasionally split the network, which meant he would show one game in North Carolina, Virginia, and Maryland and another game in the southern part of the network. For that particular split broadcast, he was showing Clemson–South Carolina in the southern part. Charlie Harville did the play-by-play, and he invited me to ride with him to Columbia. He did his 6 P.M. show, we ate dinner at his house, and then we drove to Columbia and checked into the hotel. I don't remember many details from that game, but I definitely remember the experience with Charlie.

Understand, that was a different era. When I started doing color on the broadcasts, it was so easy to get access to the coaches and players that I'd go out on the playing floor before the game and meet with the five starters and the head coach. I'd introduce the starters individually, and then I'd have one question for the head coach. Then we'd go do the same thing for the other team. Can you imagine that today? Picture Dick Vitale trying to limit himself to one question for Roy Williams or Mike Krzyzewski in the minutes before their teams tip off.

Initially, Jim Simpson and Charlie Harville were the ACC basketball broadcast team. Then Jim moved to NBC Sports, and Dan Daniel became the new play-by-play man. When I first got the opportunity from Ches to do a couple of ACC basketball games on television, I thought I had really arrived. Being part of that broadcast had been one of my goals since the time I worked at Channel 4.

It also gave me the opportunity to get more insight into ACC basketball. Today, the coaches from the league get together so fans can see them all talk about what's best for the league and about how they respect each other. When I started doing games on TV, if anybody had respect for anybody else, they never voiced it. There was much more of a sense of anger and bitterness. Much of that came from the departure of Frank McGuire, because when he left Carolina he basically told everyone off—and that included ACC commissioner Jim Weaver. It probably seemed like the logical thing for him to do because he didn't think he'd ever be back in the ACC. He was a New York City guy who was going to the bright lights of professional basketball. As it turned out, though, he was with the Warriors for only one season before they moved to California.

When South Carolina hired him, it was quite a surprise for the rest of the league. His father had been a New York City policeman, so McGuire always had that fighter's attitude. He was going to get you before you had a chance to get him. His teams in Columbia were good, but they were also physical, and they played with an attitude that let you know you'd have to beat them up in order to beat them.

I wouldn't say the eight coaches in the league disliked each other. But McGuire certainly lit the fire that made it more contentious. Everyone got along fine with Bill Gibson because everyone beat Virginia. The State-Carolina rivalry and the Duke-Carolina rivalry were always there. South Carolina and Maryland had a big fight at a game in Columbia.

We did a TV game in Columbia when Carolina played down there. George Karl was on defense in the corner. We didn't have headset microphones like broadcasters wear today. We had a table with cone-shaped microphones in front of us, and Karl was right there. He ended up on the floor, and John Ribock of South Carolina came over and kicked him in the ribs. UNC's Steve Previs came running from across the court, and you could hear him screaming in our microphones, "Did you see that? Did you tell them what he did?" There wasn't a lot we could say. In those days, only two officials worked the games, and neither one called a foul. In my opinion, it wasn't how basketball was supposed to be played, and it was a detriment to the league.

For whatever reason, it always felt like there was more resentment in ACC basketball than in ACC football. You'd sometimes run across ACC football coaches who remained friends and carried on good relationships. That rarely happened in basketball. Dean Smith and Bill Foster had been good friends when Foster was at Utah. When Foster was hired at Duke in 1974, I asked Coach Smith how it changed their relationship. "Well," he said, "Linnea and I don't get invited for dinner as much as we used to." That was the tone of the league in those days.

Despite the animosity—or maybe because of it—some memorable basketball was played in the ACC, and I was lucky enough to be at the broadcast table for some of those games. I was there for the game N.C. State won 12–10 over Duke in the 1968 ACC Tournament semifinals. Our broadcast position was on the baseline, which would cause today's television crews to go crazy. As we sat there, State was holding the ball and Duke wasn't coming out to press. Norman Prevatte, our TV director, was in a bind. There were no dead-ball situations, which meant we had no opportunities to run a commercial. Finally, Norman made the decision that we would go to commercial with the ball in play.

When we cut to commercial, N.C. State's Bill Kretzer was standing at the top of the foul circle dribbling the basketball. When we came back, he was standing at the top of the foul circle dribbling the basketball. Jim Thacker was doing play-by-play, Bones McKinney was the analyst, and I was doing the color.

Jim said, "Bones, what's happened while we were in the break?"

Bones replied, "Well, Kretzer has dribbled the ball 52 times."

Just to show what could happen in the ACC, though, we were sitting in that same broadcast position the next year when Charles Scott scored 40 points for Carolina in a comeback championship-game victory over Duke. We went from wondering if anyone would ever score one year to watching one of the greatest scoring performances in Carolina history the next year. Duke led 53–42 in the second half, but Scott finished with 28 points that half and shot 17 of 23 from the field. Duke's head coach, Vic Bubas, later talked about that game in an ACC Tournament highlight program. "Somebody's not going to like this, but I'm going to tell the truth," he said. "I looked down at the Carolina bench, and I felt everybody except Charles Scott looked like the thing was over. He was yelling, 'Give the ball to me, and I'll win the game!' And I'm afraid that's what happened." It was such an incredible performance that no Tar Heel hit 40 in the ACC Tournament again until Harrison Barnes did it in my last league tournament, the 2011 event in Greensboro, when he scored 40 against Clemson.

I was in Winston-Salem in 1967 the night that Larry Miller beat Wake Forest for the Tar Heels. In those days, you heard quite a bit about Miller, including a rumor that he had been a gang leader in his hometown of Catasauqua, Pennsylvania. He had quite a reputation on campus. But when he put on the UNC jersey, he was an incredible competitor. Bob Lewis and Miller were known as "the L&M Boys." Lewis was a great competitor also, but what you noticed first with him was his scoring ability. There was never any question with Miller that what caught your eye was the fact that he was totally unwilling to lose a game. On that particular night, Rusty Clark tipped in a miss to tie the score at 74 with less than 20 seconds to play. Wake Forest brought the ball upcourt with a chance to win, but Miller stole the ball at half court, made a twisting layup, and kept running all the way to the locker room. That was the type of play he would make for his team.

Watching so many great basketball games was enjoyable for the sports fan in me, but it was even more valuable professionally. Working with WFMY, I was getting good experience producing on deadline. We had a production manager at the station who used to constantly tell me my scripts were too late. I tried to explain that what I was talking about on the 11 P.M. sports segment might have happened just a few minutes earlier. It wasn't like I was the news anchor and could screen my film at 10 P.M. and then sit back with my feet on the desk until it was time to go on the air. There were times I'd run down the hall, toss a bit of film at the projectionist, and go straight to the set. It was nerve-racking, but it was also exhilarating.

I felt it was important to work as hard as I possibly could to prove I was capable of doing the job. I was following Charlie Harville, who had just moved nearby to WGHP in High Point. Charlie had been on television since Channel 2 came on the air in 1949. He was an icon, and I was some guy less than a year out of college who was going to take over for him. Viewers had over a decade of history with Charlie and weren't so sure they were going to necessarily translate that history to me. In many ways, I was in the same situation that Jones Angell is now in at Carolina.

Being prepared was a constant battle. Mondays meant driving to Durham to talk with the Duke football coach and, hopefully, a player for the 6 p.m. and 11 p.m. shows. Sometimes, I'd leave Durham and drive to Raleigh to get some N.C. State material. Tuesday was the day to drive to Chapel Hill. Wake Forest's media availability was on Thursday. And if football wasn't enough, there was NASCAR qualifying in Charlotte.

Once I started doing ACC games on television, I had to balance the preparation for WFMY with the preparation for the basketball games. My experience with Guilford College turned out to be helpful because it allowed me to keep practicing how to get ready for a game. I had grown up a Carolina fan. Those who knew me already understood that, but I never wanted viewers to think of me as a "Carolina guy." That might sound funny now, to think of Woody Durham as a neutral ACC observer, but I tried to make sure that was how I came across. On games for the ACC Network, we wore blue blazers and gray slacks and most of the time blue shirts, because white shirts created too much glare on TV. I always was careful to wear a tie that did not have the colors of either team. My hunch is that's partly how the ACC office became largely green and gold, because those were the most neutral colors for the eight teams.

Preparation has changed a great deal in the Internet era. Now, if I want to read a story from the *Atlanta Journal-Constitution*, I just go on-line. When I started, if I wanted to read a story from the Atlanta paper, I had to drive to Atlanta. By the time I moved full-time to Carolina games,

I subscribed to seven different newspapers. I had a clip file on every team, and I'd add to the files each day. When it was time to do a game for a team, I had a file with a season's worth of information.

Technically, the broadcasts were very different from today's. When I go back and look at old tapes, the number-one thing that sticks out to me is the on-screen graphics. In those days, we called them "supers"—those graphics at the bottom of the screen with information about the players. When I did television, those graphics would take up a third of the screen, and that was only for a player's name, height, weight, and hometown. Contrast that to today, when every game has the score constantly on the screen, plus the down and distance, scores from other games, the play clock, the game clock, and who made the most recent play and how many yards it gained. It makes us look like we were doing games in the era of the covered wagon, and now everyone is riding in sports cars.

The reason the broadcasts are able to provide that volume of information is because they're much more demanding about what they need to do a game. Today, almost every ACC football and basketball coach has a weekly press conference, plus they'll spend 10 minutes on the ACC teleconference with writers from around the country. When they have an upcoming game on TV, they'll spend time with that broadcast crew. It hasn't been that way forever. When I was looking for an interview for the 6 P.M. or 11 P.M. sports show at WFMY, I had to call and line up something individually with a coach. Very seldom did coaches have a news conference the day before a game unless it was a very big game, a bowl game, or the NCAA Tournament. That might sound like a pain to today's broadcasters, but in some ways it was helpful to me. If I had a question about why a coach ran a certain play, or about the specifics of the offense or defense, I had to schedule an interview and go find out for myself. It made me more efficient in my game preparation.

As I got settled in my roles both at WFMY and doing the ACC basketball games, it would have been hard to picture myself ever doing anything else—and that included Carolina games. I was on my way to the goals I had set during college. But things changed. In my second season, Ches decided we were going to split the games. To this day, I have always felt Dick Andrews, a vice president for Pilot Life Insurance in Greensboro, a major network sponsor, had a voice in the decision. I would do play-by-play for one half, and Jim Thacker would do it for the other half. If I did the first half this week, I'd do the second half next week. Usually, by that point, we were also picking up a weeknight game. For some reason, we didn't split that game.

But splitting the weekend games was not an ideal situation. It wasn't ideal for the viewers because they heard two different styles in the same game. Around the time they got used to one style, it changed after halftime. It wasn't ideal for Jim and me either. It had been a big deal when Jim joined the network. He was supposed to be "the guy," and now he was sharing with what I'm sure he thought was some unknown kid. He was from West Virginia and didn't have much background in ACC sports before being hired by the network. I imagine it was a little threatening to all of a sudden have to share time with me, who had been raised in the footprint of the conference and thought my dream job was to get the chair he was occupying.

The situation reached its nadir in the spring of 1971. We went into our production meeting before the championship game between Carolina and South Carolina not knowing who was going to do play-by-play. In the meeting, Ches said, "Jim, you're doing play-by-play tonight, and Woody will handle color." That ticked me off. Of course, that game turned out to be the famous—or infamous, depending on who is telling the story—jump-ball game, when six-foot-three Kevin Joyce outjumped six-foot-ten Lee Dedmon on a late-game jump ball to help the Gamecocks get the win.

It wasn't the most satisfying way to end the broadcast season. I thought that was the last game I would do that season. No one expected that in the middle of doing the ACC games, Jim would take the Duke radio play-by-play job. That left him unable to do the Carolina-Duke game in the semifinals of the 1971 NIT. At that point, the NIT was still a prestigious event. Only 16 teams made the NCAA Tournament, so the field left for the NIT was talented. In fact, Carolina had to defeat one of the greatest players of all time, Julius "Dr. J" Erving, in its first-round game

Woody and Jean with members of UNC's 1971 NIT championship team after a ceremony honoring them during the 2010–11 season
PERSONAL COLLECTION

against Massachusetts. The Tar Heels beat Providence to advance to the semifinals, which were held in New York.

That Carolina-Duke contest was the last game I ever did on television. Fittingly, the Tar Heels won it, 73–67, and went on to win the NIT title. And it might have been even more fitting that the entire 1971 team was honored at the Smith Center at halftime of a game during my final season behind the microphone, 2011. All of us had come a long way since that night in New York.

The way the ACC season ended, with Jim Thacker doing the entire championship game, left me a little sour. It's not accurate to say I went out job hunting in the summer of 1971. But it's not inaccurate to say I was slightly more open to possibilities than I otherwise might have been. Remember, I still had a job broadcasting ACC basketball games and was still on track to achieve what had been my long-term goal for many years. I wasn't in a bad situation. The radio play-by-play job opening at Carolina helped me consider new opportunities.

Many people don't realize that my departure from ACC games brought Billy Packer into their living rooms. Bones McKinney came back to the network, but Ches also added Packer as an analyst. Billy became almost synonymous with the league, but it never felt like he really endeared himself to fans. Working with NBC turned out to be a tremendous break for him because being teamed with Dick Enberg and Al McGuire created some chemistry. Al was likely to say anything. And Billy was more of the straight man but completely believed everything he said. At the time I left, none of us had any idea what was to come. We didn't know we'd be working together for decades. When he did ACC games, Al would always stop by our booth and ask for a nugget about each Carolina player that he could use in the broadcast.

When I left, I didn't know Billy would join the network. I just knew it appealed to me that at Carolina I wouldn't have to split anything. I assumed Jim and I would go right back to splitting the ACC games the next season, and that was getting old. Even after I started doing Carolina games, I still had a small feeling of missing out on some of the big TV games. In particular, the N.C. State–Maryland game on Super Sunday in 1973 was a significant national game. Ches convinced 145 stations across the country to join the network for that game, State had a phenom named David Thompson, and both teams were ranked in the national top five. It was exactly the kind of game I had always dreamed of doing for the ACC Network. An estimated 25 million people watched it. State won, 87–85.

That day, I might have felt a twinge of regret that I wasn't setting up courtside at Cole Field House. But the incredible ride I was about to begin in Chapel Hill made me forget all my television dreams.

Memorable Moments

March 17, 1990 | Carolina 79, Oklahoma 77 (NCAA Tournament second round)

"Eight seconds remain, score tied at 77. Nate Humphrey hands King Rice the ball, pushes it in to Hubert Davis. Eight seconds. Davis trying to get free, over to Fox. Fox baseline, up for the shot, good! Off the glass. Oklahoma calls timeout, but the game is over, the game is over! Carolina has upset number-one Oklahoma! . . . They played the Sooners right off their feet. And there is justice in Austin, Texas!"

An incident before the game stuck out in my mind. I did my pregame interview at the hotel in Austin four hours before the pregame meal. When I arrived at Coach Smith's room to do the interview, he was watching tape of the Sooners playing against Kansas. He had about five minutes of tape left to watch because he wanted to see a specific play. As he shut the television off, he put the remote down on the coffee table. He turned to me and said, "I think I know them pretty well. Now, if I can just communicate it to the team." When Rick Fox made that shot, that's the first thing that came to my mind—he obviously was able to communicate it to the team very well.

Chapter 5

Voice of the Tar Heels

In February of 1971, Bill Currie left his job as the radio play-by-play man at North Carolina. He'd been broadcasting the Tar Heels and the Carolina Cougars, which was interesting because you could fit what Bill knew about pro basketball—and particularly the ABA—on the head of a pin. Bob Lamey came in and finished the 1970–71 basketball season, but most of us in the business knew the job would be open going into the spring.

One day, I got a phone call at Channel 2 from Carolina athletic director Homer Rice. He said, "I want you to come have lunch with me tomorrow because I'd like to talk to you about our radio situation."

I had no interest. I wanted to continue doing games on television and eventually have a shot at being the Atlantic Coast Conference's primary play-by-play man. I understood that I'd have to bide my time until I got older to have a shot at the full-time position. And while I understood that, it just so happened that the spring of 1971 was a frustrating time because I was tired of splitting the basketball games. Preparation was difficult when we often didn't know until the day of the game who would do play-by-play and who would do color. The combination of that uncertainty and the fact that Homer Rice had always been nice to me led me to say I would meet him.

The next day, I walked into his office, and he said, "I found out something interesting about you yesterday."

"What was that?" I asked him.

I'll never forget what he said next: "I found out that you went to school here."

I took that as a great compliment, and that's exactly what I told him: "Homer, if I've been doing ACC basketball for four years and you didn't know until yesterday that I went to school at Carolina, I've been doing a heck of a job."

We had a big laugh over it, and he took me to lunch at The Pines. As we sat there, I didn't have much interest in the position. I listened to what he said about some of the requirements of the job, but I still thought of myself as a television guy.

But as I drove back to Greensboro down Highway 54, the more I thought about it, the more interested I became.

I did my 6 P.M. sports show and went home for dinner. I had already talked to Jean on the telephone—just think, I had to wait until I got back to Greensboro to call her, rather than contacting her on the way home from a cell phone—but sitting down for dinner was our first chance to really discuss the details. Of course, we didn't know at the time that we were talking about a job I would hold for 40 years. But we did recognize it was a change. It would take me off the path I thought I wanted to follow.

Finally, Jean said, "If you don't try for this, you may look back on it with regret at some point in your career."

That made sense to me. It also made me want to fully invest myself in trying to get the job.

I called both Coach Dean Smith and Coach Bill Dooley and asked if they would support me if I became an official candidate for the job, and they indicated they would. The next day, I talked to Homer on the phone and told him how much the job had been on my mind, and that I'd like to pursue it.

It wasn't a true case of switching jobs, since I was adding the Carolina play-by-play duties to my existing job at Channel 2. That meant I had to clear it with the station, since it was my primary employer. If it had been any school other than Carolina, I don't think the station would have been willing to let me do it. In fact, Skeeter Francis once called and asked if I'd be interested in the Wake Forest play-by-play job for football and basketball, and Channel 2 nixed it. If it had been a school other than Carolina, I would have been forced to make a difficult decision: leave Channel 2 to pursue a play-by-play job or stay and miss out on play-by-play. However, Carolina carried weight in the state, and some connections were in place, so the station was agreeable to letting me pursue both. It was announced that spring, shortly before I went on an outing at Wrightsville Beach with about eight guys—including Bill Dooley—and their wives. My memory is that the decision received a positive response. Then again, I don't know if people who didn't like the idea would have walked up to me and said, "Ol' Woody will never be able to pull this off."

When Bill Currie left, the UNC network changed rights-holders. The rights were picked up by G. H. Johnston, an advertising agency in New York. It was the big Texaco ad agency and had rights for a number of schools in the South, including Georgia. The arrangement was unique. For one game, Texaco would have all the commercial breaks in the first half and the local affiliates would have all the second-half breaks. The next week, they'd switch the format, with the local stations getting the first-half commercials and Texaco moving to the second half.

As I got into my early years on the job, I didn't have as many conflicts with my Channel 2 work as might be expected. In the ACC, most of the trips were driveable, so I could do my 11 P.M. sports show on Friday and then drive to wherever the game would be played the next day. My first conflict was a memorable one. It came in 1972, when Dooley won a second straight ACC championship. The team wrapped up a 14-week regular season in the Gator Bowl against Florida. That same night, a Carolina–Virginia Tech basketball game was played in Charlotte.

Coach Dooley wanted to get back to Chapel Hill even though he let the team stay in Jacksonville overnight, so we came back immediately. We had a private jet, and everyone on the plane was celebrating because the

Tar Heels had just won a tight 28–24 game against the Gators. The situation was going to work out perfectly—win the football game, get back as quickly as possible, and do a basketball game the same day.

About that time, the pilot came on the intercom: "Charlotte has just dropped below minimums. We can't land right now. The controllers tell us it could open up again at any minute."

We circled the Charlotte airport three times. One of the WBT radio guys was sitting at the Charlotte Coliseum, ready to go on the air as our backup. Finally, we heard the pilot again: "We're going to make one more attempt. If we can't land, we have to go to Raleigh-Durham for fuel."

It got quiet on that plane. It was still foggy. Suddenly, we saw lights underneath us getting brighter. A couple of seconds later, the wheels hit the runway. As we got our stuff out of the plane, no one was quite sure how we pulled it off. Then we were told a navy trainer had come in right before us and that we tucked in behind it and landed. I was able to do the game at the coliseum, fly back to RDU, and record Coach Smith's television show the next morning.

That time, the overlap wasn't enough to prevent us from doing both games. But sometimes, especially as the basketball season began tipping off earlier and earlier, it was impossible to do both. In total, I missed 14 basketball games because of conflicts with football.

The foggy night in Charlotte wasn't the most indelible image from my first couple years on the job. That came in my very first game as Carolina's play-by-play broadcaster, which followed the death of Bill Arnold in football practice from heat prostration. To this day, there are many different opinions about what could have caused his death. John Bunting, one of Bill's teammates, still doesn't talk openly about it. No one blamed Bill Dooley, but there was harsh criticism of how hard some of the assistant coaches were pushing the players.

John was right there when it happened. At that point in the practice, the vehicles used to carry coaches and items between the practice field and the field house were already gone. Some of them had even taken back players bothered by the heat. So John had to pick Bill up and put him on the truck. First, he was carried to the old field house to see John Lacey, the trainer. Immediately, Lacey knew Bill had to go to the hospital, where Bill died during the middle of the week before the first game of the season, which was to be played at Richmond.

It might seem strange that a program like Carolina would play a road game at Richmond. E. Claiborne Robins, a pharmaceutical executive in Richmond, was determined to get ACC teams to play in his city and was willing to pay the guarantee himself. It was a night game at City Stadium, and we had a meeting in an empty dining room at the team hotel to decide how we were going to address Bill Arnold's death. It was decided I would read a statement on the air about the sadness of the week, his attributes as a person, and his potential as a player. We wanted to recognize the situation without calling even more attention to it.

Coach Dooley's house was the usual gathering spot after games. That same month, I was in his kitchen after a home game, and Bill Arnold's father was there. It was a trying time for Dooley because he was getting significant criticism. An on-campus group was using Bill Richardson, a former football player, as its mouthpiece to speak out against the football program. It got so heated that Bill Arnold's family offered to issue a statement absolving Coach Dooley. He refused, telling the Arnold family it had been through enough.

The situation finally came to an end when the Richardson-led group had a news conference in the student union. Virtually the entire football team walked from Navy Field to the student union in full practice gear, and Coach Dooley challenged Richardson on some of the statements he was presenting as fact that actually were not true.

During John Bunting's tenure as head coach, he brought the Arnold family back to Chapel Hill. They stood down by the tunnel as the team ran onto the field, and the program presented them with a jersey with Bill's number on it. It's hard to believe it took over 30 years for them to receive closure from the program.

The best advice I received came early in my work for Carolina: "Don't try to be Bill Currie." I had already made that decision on my own because

I knew that what made him good was his unique humor and down-home approach. I knew I couldn't do it the same way and make it sound authentic. I made a conscious decision that I would do it my way and let the listeners decide if that worked for them.

I did inherit Bill's spotters, which was a fantastic break. He used twin brothers, the Bowens, who had played for Catawba. Carroll would handle Carolina, while Harold did the visiting team. They called me before I ever had a chance to contact them and said they would be interested in continuing. I was so thankful to get that call because they were really good at what they did. Carroll worked with us only about three years before he had some back problems—in those days, doing football games meant climbing a lot of steps to get to the press box. Harold brought in Whitey Smith for a few years. But once it got too cramped in the booth, Harold began spotting for both teams. He was with me for 30 years. Eventually, knee problems forced him to stop doing the games. His wife, Jean, was concerned about all the walking we had to do. It was painful to have to tell him I thought it was time for him to give it up, not just because he was such a longtime member of the crew but because I appreciated how good he was at his job.

The spotting job is one fans might not understand or appreciate. Even some people in the radio business don't appreciate it. They think having a spotter is a luxury—and I guess it is, if you don't care too much about the quality of the broadcast and want only the basics. So much happens on any given football play. While the play-by-play man is calling the action involving the ball carrier, it is impossible to see which defender is applying pressure to the quarterback or who the first man in on the tackle might have been. That's where a good spotter can help, since he knows what you need even before you need it. When it works right, it's seamless on the air—call the play, call the ball carrier, call the yardage, then describe some of the players who were also integral to the play. I was fortunate that I had help later in my career from Eric Fiddleman, Jody Zeugner, and Greg Tilley, who were all good. We were able to develop some of the same chemistry I had with Harold.

In his first year as the voice of the Tar Heels, Woody worked with Bob Quincy, the former sports editor of the Charlotte News.

It was a painful change for everyone involved when Bill Dooley was replaced by Dick Crum. Dooley's postgame celebrations with friends and family had become legendary. The Pines had an upstairs room where everyone would gather for dinner. The coaching staff, their wives, and former players all had an open invitation. You never knew who you might see. Once Crum arrived, all that ended. After a game, he went home to bed. That was a big change in the overall feel of the program. Some people never adjusted to the difference.

Greensboro alumnus Joe Maddux headed the search committee that hired Crum, who was recommended by Dr. Carl Blyth, a committee member and UNC professor of exercise and sport science. After four years at Miami of Ohio, where his teams won 76 percent of their games, Crum, who was not a Miami alum, never really felt accepted at the Cradle of Coaches, which led him to apply for the Carolina job.

The committee mandated that all eligible candidates must apply. Rumors persisted that Nebraska's Tom Osborne was interested in the position but was not going to officially apply. In his first five years, his Cornhuskers had won 75 percent of their games. He coached another successful 20 years in Lincoln before getting into politics and then returning as the school's athletic director. It's entirely possible that if the committee had dropped the application requirement, Osborne could have been a real candidate for Carolina's next football coach.

Crum did show me that he was a smart football coach. In his first season, he ran a draw play to Amos Lawrence that was a brilliant call. And I believe his 1980 team didn't get enough national attention because of the lopsided nature of its loss to Oklahoma, which was the Tar Heels' only defeat of the season. The team still finished with a win over Texas in the Bluebonnet Bowl at Houston's Astrodome, which was an impressive end to the season. But nationally, I'm not sure how many people realized how good Carolina was that year.

Around the end of that season, Crum began to loosen up a little bit. He was nice enough to invite Jean and me to spend some time at his family cabin on a lake in Canada. It was so beautiful that we taped his first television show for 1981 at the cabin. He was comfortable in the mountains.

One day, we were out on his boat fishing, and he asked, "Is anybody hungry?" His three boys were with us, and of course boys are always hungry, so they said they could use something to eat. Crum docked on one of the many islands in Lake Temagami, grabbed his fishing reel, cast into the water, caught a fish, pulled it out, filleted it on a boat paddle, and there was lunch.

"Coach," I told him after watching him catch several more, "I see now what you meant when you said you'd be a forest ranger if you weren't a football coach."

Interacting warmly with people just didn't come naturally to Dick Crum. And as being a football coach became even more about meeting with donors and selling the program, the job wasn't a great fit for his personality. By the time he realized he needed to make an effort to be more friendly, it was too late, as fans and donors had already formed an opinion of him based on how he'd acted previously. He had a preference for recruiting in the Midwest, especially in Ohio, and of course Carolina was going to get only the Midwest players that Michigan and Ohio State and the rest of the Big Ten didn't want. By the time Crum left, the joke was that Carolina had an average Mid-American Conference football team.

That shortchanged his early tenure. He inherited Lawrence Taylor, who remains one of the most exciting players I've ever seen on a football field. Dooley had moved Taylor around to several positions, and Crum did also. In his junior year, Taylor began to emerge. The game in Raleigh against N.C. State was the trigger for him. He was involved in a huge quarterback sack that forced a fumble near the goal line. After the game, I went into the locker room, and the media was crowded so thickly around him I couldn't even get to him. That was his first step toward becoming who we now know as Lawrence Taylor, the Hall of Fame football player.

When he came back for his senior year, he was the most dominant player I'd ever seen to that point. Younger fans like to talk about Julius Peppers as a physical freak. Taylor was the original. A lot of stories were told about what he was doing off the field—the most famous involved him climbing up the outside of Ehringhaus Dorm—but on the field it was hard to stop him. He later told me he felt the Clemson game during his senior year, when he had a big sack to preserve the win, was the highlight of his college career. "That's what probably got me the attention that turned me into a first-round draft choice," he said.

Three seasons into my tenure as Carolina's play-by-play broadcaster, the Tar Heels played the legendary game against Duke at Carmichael Auditorium that included a comeback from eight points down in 17 seconds. Nearly 40 years later, that game has endured like no other nonchampionship game in Carolina history. Without fail, when I do talks and ask fans to mention one game that is more significant to them than any other—with the exception of championship games—someone will mention that game. And in their next breath, they'll talk about Walter Davis's incredible shot to tie the game at the end of regulation. Bill Guthridge said it best: "One hundred thousand people say they saw that shot, and Carmichael was about half full when he made it."

I could understand why our fans would want to leave early. Duke wasn't good that year, and no one wanted to hang around and watch its team celebrate at Carmichael. Carolina players still talk reverently about the mood on the bench in the closing moments of that game. It was as if Coach Smith orchestrated every play. During the timeouts, he'd say, "Okay, guys, we're going to steal the inbounds pass." The game unfolded exactly as he predicted—and he was the only one anywhere who could ever have predicted that. How do you explain that type of comeback with no three-point shot?

We taped Coach Smith's television show that same night, after the game. He liked to have the game tape edited with our radio broadcast audio over the top because he wanted to hear the crowd's reaction to certain plays. Until I walked in to record his show, I honestly couldn't remember what I said when Davis's shot banked off the glass and through the net. But what else could I have called it except "un-bee-lievable"?

Not everyone is quite as reverent about the comeback. I did a talk in Roanoke Rapids one year. Afterward, some fans were nice enough to come talk to me. One guy finally worked his way over and said, "Let me get this straight. Carolina had Bobby Jones on the floor?"

"That's right," I said.

"And Mitch Kupchak?"

"Yes, Mitch was on that team." I thought maybe he was trying to remember the roster.

"Walter Davis was playing then?"

"Well, yes, he made the game-tying shot."

The man looked at me again. "What I want to know," he said, "is how Carolina got behind by eight points with that team on the court."

That was the first time since 1974 anyone ever asked me that question, and that game has been brought up to me regularly over the past 38 years.

The environment in Carmichael was so unique. The students had all the grandstands up against the wall of Woollen Gym. When you watched a game there, you felt like you were in the game. You can still occasionally get that same feeling at the Smith Center, but it doesn't happen as frequently as it did at Carmichael.

Everyone talks about how hot it was in there. Coach Smith sometimes got the blame for the temperature. His wife, Linnea, once said, "He doesn't even know where the heat controls are at home. How would he know how to turn up the heat at Carmichael?"

I looked at the huddle one time from the broadcast perch in Carmichael—I had an elevated spot and could look almost straight down into the huddle—and Coach Smith was wearing a three-piece wool suit with the vest. As you can imagine, he looked hot. I said on the air, "Coach Smith told me a long time ago he never perspires during a game, but he really perspires after the game." The team was just coming out of a time-out, and he did that move where he brushed his hair back off his forehead. With that suit, and the small arena, and the fans right on top of him, it was obvious he was hot. "I think he just wiped some of his imagination right off his forehead," I said.

Coach Smith had a way of letting you know when he didn't agree with something. In the spring of 1972, Carolina was preparing to play Florida State in the Final Four. When we got the lineups, Bobby Jones was listed as a starter instead of Bill Chamberlain. That was a significant change, and I handled it the wrong way. I went down to the bench, where the team was finishing pregame warmups, and asked Coach Smith why the lineup was changed. I will never forget his response: "That's none of your business."

The subject was never mentioned again, but I learned something really important that day. In a game situation, a head coach's attention is on his team. That's not the time to do anything to take him out of his routine. On the air, I simply said, "Bobby Jones is getting the start tonight. Apparently, something has happened. Perhaps Bill was late for a pregame meal."

It all seemed pretty easy my first year in the booth. The football team won the ACC championship, the basketball team went to the Final Four for the fourth time in six years, and ol' Woody sounded really smart on the radio.

Two years later, we had the "eight points in 17 seconds" game, and the next season the Tar Heels added a freshman point guard named Phil Ford. The first time I saw him play was in the state 4A championship game at Greensboro Grimsley High School. In a surge right before half-time, he stole two inbounds passes and scored about 10 points in a span of roughly 60 seconds. I remember thinking, Holy cow! He was as quick as a cat. If you were running with him while trying to defend him on the break, you weren't going to catch him. His physical talent was impressive. Phil never, ever showed any emotion. He'd drive in and get past the defense for a layup. Before I had time to describe what happened, he'd be back at midcourt with his hand up, calling the defense.

I believe that if you asked ACC basketball fans to write down the five best players ever in the league, Phil Ford would get the majority of the votes at point guard. He has a special place not only at Carolina but in the conference. And what he did in Chapel Hill has been repaid by Coach Smith, who kept a special eye out for him for many years. We all know Coach Smith would never name his favorite players. That's totally opposite of everything he stands for. But with all those two went through together, it's easy to see they had such a special relationship.

Memorable Moments

March 2, 1974 | Carolina 96, Duke 92 (OT)

"Kupchak will make the long frontcourt pass. Gets it to Walter Davis, two . . . one . . . Walter takes the shot. It's good! The game is tied! Un-bee-lievable!"

I didn't know I'd said, "Un-bee-lievable!" until I did Coach Smith's television show and heard the call. When I played in charity golf tournaments that spring, little boys would come running across the course screaming, "Un-bee-lievable!"

Before the "eight points in 17 seconds" situation started unfolding, I was already setting the scene for a Carolina loss—what the records would be, how the seedings would look going into the ACC Tournament—and giving Duke credit for the win. When Walter let the shot go, my first instinct was that it was too strong. Mentally, I was getting ready to say, "Well, it's been a great comeback, but it just came up a little bit short." Then, boom, it banked in.

Comebacks like that one helped build the uniqueness of the Carolina basketball program and the belief in opponents that they were never quite sure they had the Tar Heels beaten.

Chapter 6

National Champions

The 1982 championship season actually began on the last night of the 1980–81 season. On March 30, 1981, the Tar Heels arrived at the Philadelphia Spectrum to play Indiana for the national title. Except that no one knew if they were actually going to play. The first thing someone said to me when I walked into the arena was, "Hey, we may not play this game."

Earlier in the day, a would-be assassin shot President Ronald Reagan. As late as an hour before the game, we didn't know if the teams were going to play. The consolation game between Virginia and LSU was played, but the nine-man NCAA Tournament Committee was still in discussions between the two games about whether it was appropriate to play a championship basketball game. Imagine playing a game and finding out during the action that the president had died. Today, everyone would get minute-by-minute updates on his health. In 1981, it wasn't that easy. It was known that the president was in recovery from surgery. Eventually, the committee—led by Wayne Duke, the Big 10 commissioner—received the go-ahead to play.

By that point, the players were already on the floor warming up. It was an awkward situation. Of course, since Carolina lost, fans might look back and wonder, *What if the teams had waited until the next night to play?* I've always believed, however, that the key part of that matchup with Indiana was the fact that the Tar Heels had beaten the Hoosiers earlier in the season. Sometimes, winning those early-season matchups can come back to haunt you in a later meeting. That's what happened in 1981 and also in 1993, when Michigan beat Carolina in Hawaii and then the Tar Heels beat the Wolverines for the national championship.

In terms of world events, the storyline of the 1981 title game was the situation involving President Reagan. In the basketball world, the story was the matchup between Indiana's Bob Knight and Carolina's Dean Smith. People think of them as very different. But even by 1981, they already had a close relationship. Early in his career, Coach Knight called Coach Smith regarding the motion offense. Coach Knight used that offense with his 1976 undefeated championship team, and Coach Smith said the way that Indiana team ran the motion offense was one of the best he'd ever seen. Technically, they were both smart. They also knew each other well, so there was some level of being able to predict what the other was going to do. Everyone could see the personality differences. Coach Knight was more volatile on the bench, but Coach Smith certainly wasn't a wallflower either.

When Indiana won that 1981 title game 63–50, it was Knight's second championship, and Coach Smith had been to six Final Fours without a title. This sounds crazy today, but the national perception of Coach Smith at that time was that he was a good coach but couldn't win the big game. Of course, those of us close to the program knew how ridiculous that was. Couldn't win the big game? How many big games did he have to win just to get to that last big game at the end of the season?

In my opinion, the one missed opportunity of those first six tries that still hurts the most was the 1977 loss to Marquette. Overcoming all the injuries endured by that Carolina team was remarkable. As the Tar Heels kept winning through all the setbacks—Tom LaGarde was hurt, Walter Davis was hurt, Phil Ford was hurt—at some point I just decided, *Well, this team is destined to win.* Even with all the injuries, Carolina was a better team than Marquette that season. Those involved say losing that national championship game still hurts even 35 years later. Emotionally, the players felt they let Coach Smith down. The story is that after the loss, Coach Smith went around the locker room taking soft drinks to the players, trying to console them. That's a heartbreaking image.

In some ways, the feeling was similar after 1981, although it wasn't as pronounced. The players knew after the 1981 runner-up finish that Coach Smith was going to be a story. He was aware of what people were saying but would never, ever let you know. The players knew, though. All the major contributors from 1981 with the exception of Al Wood were coming back. The players didn't know the incoming freshman named Mike Jordan would turn out to be Michael Jordan, but they knew they were going to have a competitive team. By the time they got back to Chapel Hill from Philadelphia, they were already motivated to return to the Final Four and win it all.

That group had remarkable chemistry. Intramural softball was a big deal around Chapel Hill at that time, and the basketball team formed a softball team that would absolutely smash people. I felt that as long as everyone stayed healthy over the summer and throughout the next season, the team had a good chance of contending for the title.

A talented freshman class was also coming in. In the fall of 1981, Coach Smith and I attended an event on campus at which he made some short remarks. I drove him back to Carmichael Auditorium. I said, "Coach, how's practice going?"

He said, "Well, pretty good."

Of course, I knew that James Worthy and Jimmy Black and Matt Doherty and Sam Perkins were back, and there was no question about how good they were.

That's when Coach Smith made the greatest understatement of all time: "I think the young man from Wilmington might be able to help us."

I remember that like it was yesterday. The young man from Wilmington was Michael Jordan, and he did turn out to be quite a help.

In the fall of 1981, though, he was not the story. Going to practice, your eye was drawn first to Worthy or Perkins because they were the

Woody with Michael Jordan at a function on the UNC campus around 1996, when Jordan gave a $1 million gift to the UNC School of Social Work

known stars. It was not unusual for Worthy to simply dominate people in practice. The things he did in games were often spectacular, but his teammates saw that every single day in Carmichael. Who had time to watch a skinny freshman play when a superstar like James Worthy was on the court? By the time the season started, there was no question it was Worthy's team. He was so mature as a leader, and he worked hard all the time. He was a great example for the younger players to follow.

It was obvious early in the season that Carolina was going to be a national championship contender again. The Tar Heels beat Kentucky in a one-versus-two game in the Meadowlands. That was the first sign.

In those days, the real measuring sticks were the games against Virginia. Duke was a rivalry because of proximity, but Virginia was a rivalry because it and Carolina were often the two best teams in the conference. UVA's coach, Terry Holland, had been an assistant coach at Maryland under Lefty Driesell, so he'd absorbed all that animosity—some people might call it jealousy—toward Carolina from the Terrapins. When Holland got a chance to have his own ACC team, he carried that with him to Charlottesville.

The flashpoint was the recruitment of Ralph Sampson, the seven-foot-four center. The story went that the day before Sampson announced his college choice, he wore a Carolina shirt to school. Everyone assumed he was coming to Chapel Hill. When he didn't, it created quite a spark in the relationship between Carolina and Virginia. He was worth the fuss, too, because he became a three-time National Player of the Year. And yet as good as he was, he had a losing record against Carolina, including dropping two of three in 1982, when both teams were ranked in the nation's top three. That says something about how good the Tar Heels were.

After the teams split the first two meetings, each winning at home, everyone wanted to see Carolina and Virginia play again in the ACC Tournament final. That's what happened. The Tar Heels won that game 47–45. Everyone said Carolina won because it held the ball. Well, Ralph Sampson was standing under the basket. Would you want to take the ball to the rim with the nation's best shot blocker right there? Of course not. With no shot clock, the best strategy was to make him come out and play away from the basket, and that's exactly what Dean Smith did. People forget that when Virginia had to foul to get Carolina into the bonus situation, the Cavaliers had several fouls to give because they'd chosen not to come out and chase earlier in the game. That strategy backfired on them because it enabled the Tar Heels to run off a couple extra minutes of clock before they got into a free-throw situation. After the ACC Tournament, many observers thought Carolina and Virginia would meet again in the Final Four in New Orleans, but the Cavaliers didn't make it.

That Final Four might have been the most physically talented of all time. Just to get to the championship game, Carolina had to beat Houston—essentially the same Phi Slamma Jamma team that was a prohibitive favorite over N.C. State the next season. The Cougars had Clyde Drexler and Akeem Olajuwon, and no one ever even mentions that win. The other semifinal had Georgetown with Sleepy Floyd and Patrick Ewing against Louisville with Derek Smith, Rodney McCray, and Jerry Eaves. In that Final Four were five of the NBA's eventual 50 greatest players of all time—Worthy, Jordan, Ewing, Olajuwon, and Drexler—plus four Hall of Fame coaches.

Coach Smith and John Thompson of Georgetown had a relationship dating back to when Coach Smith had recruited Donald Washington, who played for Coach Thompson at St. Anthony's in Washington, D.C. The friendship deepened when Thompson took over at Georgetown in 1972. Coach Smith chose his friend as an assistant coach on the 1976 Olympic team. I believe he liked Coach Thompson and thought he was a talented young coach. They were still competitive, but there was also some mutual admiration. It was a different relationship from what Coach Smith had with some other ACC coaches at that time.

Ewing was still evolving into the player he was going to be. In the championship game, Coach Smith told his team there was a good chance Ewing might try to block everything, and that's exactly what happened. He was called for goaltending five times in the first half. Georgetown may have believed that Carolina would eventually be intimidated and stop taking the ball to the basket. In reality, the opposite happened. The Tar Heels were getting points—the ball wasn't actually going through the

From left to right are Jim Valvano, Frank McGuire, and Woody at the 1982 Final Four.
Photo by Hugh Morton

rim, but they were scoring—so why not keep taking the ball right at Ewing? I don't think there was any intimidation at all.

The other storyline of the game, in addition to Ewing trying to block everything, was the performance by Worthy. Today, everyone knows the game because of Jordan's shot. But that was Worthy's game. He shot 13 of 17 and finished with 28 points. Considering the situation and the opponent, it was among the top five performances I've ever seen from a Carolina player.

Even with that great performance by Worthy, the game was close in the final moments. Our broadcast position was more toward the Georgetown bench than the Carolina bench. Late in the game, with the Tar Heels down by one, Coach Smith called a timeout. Later, he said he could sense some uneasiness in his team. The players came to the bench and gathered around him. Then Coach Smith said to them, "We've got them right where we want them."

Roy Williams was an assistant coach on that team and remembers faking a cough so he could sneak a look at the scoreboard. He thought maybe he had lost track of the score and the Tar Heels actually were ahead. Why else would Coach Smith say they had Georgetown right where he wanted? Sure enough, though, the Hoyas had a one-point lead. The message Coach Smith was trying to get across was that Carolina had the ball with a chance to determine the winner. The team would get to decide the national champion. If it executed, the winner would be the Tar Heels.

Because Coach Thompson knew Coach Smith so well, he understood exactly what to take away first. He was not going to lose the game by allowing Carolina to get the ball inside to Worthy or Perkins. Meanwhile, Coach Smith knew that Coach Thompson knew that's what Carolina wanted to do. It was quite a chess match during that timeout. Coach Smith set up a rotation of the ball to take a look inside, but I don't think he really believed that would be open. If it was open, that would be great, but it was unlikely to be there. Coming out of the timeout huddle, that's why he slapped Jordan on the rump and said, "Knock it in, Michael." Coach Smith knew because of the way the ball would rotate and the way the players would react to that rotation that Jordan would likely end up with the ball in a scoring position. As Carolina players have said so often, they felt as if Coach Smith already knew what was going to happen before it actually did. That was certainly the case in the final 30 seconds of the 1982 championship game.

Michael made the jump shot with 17 seconds left to give Carolina a 63–62 lead. Georgetown had a timeout but didn't call it, and then Fred Brown threw the ball away to Worthy no more than 20 feet away from where I was sitting. I have absolutely no idea why Worthy was so far away from the basket on defense. I do have a theory for why Brown threw the ball. Georgetown had been the higher-seeded team all the way through the tournament, which meant they wore light-colored jerseys. In the championship game, though, the Hoyas were wearing blue jerseys. Fred Brown knew he wasn't supposed to have the ball that far from the basket. He wanted to get rid of it. He saw a flash of white and thought, *I've got to get this ball to Ewing or Floyd for the last shot*, and he got rid of it as fast as he could.

Three weeks later, I went by the basketball office. Eddie Fogler was in there watching film. I believe it was one of the first times he'd really tried to break it down. He asked me to come sit with him, and he froze the film with Brown holding the ball. Sleepy Floyd was down on the baseline, and I could see Brown wanted to make the pass to him. But Jordan was at the top of the defense and took one step to his left, which blocked the passing lane. This was before Michael was an accomplished player, because he really improved defensively for his sophomore season. But as a freshman, that one step to the left changed the entire play. One step changed the game. It makes you a little nervous to think of it that way, doesn't it?

The turnover put the ball into the hands of Worthy, who dribbled down the court. I was going into my call ("The Tar Heels are going to win the national championship!") when I looked down at the UNC bench and Coach Smith was calling everyone together, calm as usual.

Carolina had some experience with losing games in that situation. The sad part is that when you lose in the championship game, it's almost like you're in the way of the celebration everyone is trying to have. You're one of the two best teams in the country, and it's like you haven't accomplished anything. I remember thinking, *We don't have to worry about that this year.* I also remember thinking as the game was ending, *They can't say anything about Coach Smith anymore.*

I couldn't believe how calm he was. Trust me—no one else in the Superdome was that calm. One of the greatest Carolina basketball pictures ever is the Hugh Morton shot of Coach Smith, Jimmy Black, James Worthy, and sports information director Rick Brewer after the game, when they were all completely exhausted. I have that photo in my office. Someone once asked me, "Why do you have a photo of a loss on your wall?" That's how fatigued they look. It's the perfect picture of how much winning a championship can take out of you. The net around Worthy's neck is the only hint Carolina won the game.

The team stayed at a separate hotel from the fans in 1982. It was different in 1993 because everyone stayed together. It was a fantastic scene at the hotel when the players came back and people were lining the staircases and escalators to cheer them on. In 1982, though, the big celebration came back in Chapel Hill. Two planes returned home the next day. We were on the first one, and the team and support staff were on the second one. It was a gorgeous day. As we went into our landing pattern, the pilot said over the PA, "You can already see that the north side of Kenan Stadium is full."

We went straight to the stadium, and I was told I was the choice to emcee the event. It didn't exactly require a big speech. The team was about 30 minutes behind us. By the time we had everything set up, the players came through the football locker room holding the trophy, and the place went crazy for several minutes. It is always a spectacular feeling to win a championship. That one, though, was unique. It had the sense of achievement mixed with the satisfaction of doing it for Coach Smith—who was so humble he didn't even attend the welcome-home celebration because he wanted the focus to be on the players—plus the feeling of having been so close before and finally finishing the job. When the players left Kenan, the bus drove them down Franklin Street because most of them lived at Granville Towers. What a way to share the celebration with the town that had supported them all the way to the title!

That night in New Orleans, Carolina basketball changed. The only negative anyone had been able to say about Dean Smith was that he'd never won a national championship. Now, he had his title. What else could people say about him? It was obvious he was running the best program in America and had North Carolina on top of the college basketball world.

Now, of course, we know that night also introduced us to someone who would be important not just to basketball but to sports overall and maybe even to the country. Before that game, people were aware that Michael Jordan was a good freshman basketball player, but that was the extent of it. That game punched his ticket for the rest of his college career. And he kept improving. That's what people underestimate about him. It would have been easy to let that shot—it still might be the most famous in Carolina basketball history—become the pinnacle of a career. He wasn't willing to do that. He handled the immediate fame as well as any college student ever could. I never got the sense he was too impressed with himself. He kept working and kept listening to Coach Smith's advice about how to improve. By the time he left after the 1983–84 season, he was a much more complete player than he was in 1982.

Especially early in his career, he got the most attention for his dunking. Fans saw some incredible ones during his Carolina career, but none that topped the rock-the-cradle dunk at Cole Field House in the closing moments of a win over Maryland in 1984. It was a spectacular play, and he did it so effortlessly. It was the kind of moment highlight shows dream of.

Except for the Dean Smith television show, that is. The Maryland game was on a Saturday, and Coach Smith's show aired on Sunday. I felt sure we would have plenty of footage of the great dunk. Until, that is, Coach Smith specifically requested that we not show Jordan's dunk on the program. He felt it would be disrespectful to Maryland. That's how the only program in the nation not to include Jordan's dunk—which still airs as a part of ESPN's college basketball promos—was Carolina's own television show.

Memorable Moments

March 29, 1982: Carolina 63, Georgetown 62

"Doherty in the double-team, gives it back to Black with 20 seconds left to play. Goes back to Michael Jordan, jumper from out on the left . . . good! Thirteen . . . 12 . . . 11 . . . Georgetown with one timeout. Fred Brown looking— threw it away to Worthy! Worthy . . . five . . . the Tar Heels are going to win the national championship!"

Everything broke loose when Michael hit the shot. Georgetown had a timeout but didn't call it. The Hoyas brought the ball frontcourt, and I was excited about Michael making the shot, but at the same time, I was thinking, What am I going to say if Georgetown scores and Carolina loses another championship game?

As I was trying to sort all that out mentally, Fred Brown threw the ball to Worthy. James took off down the court, and I was already into, "The Tar Heels are going to win the national championship!" We were broadcasting from almost right behind the Georgetown bench, and all of a sudden at the other end I saw Coach Smith calling everybody over to him, and he knew it wasn't over. He wanted to get everyone settled for the free throws.

If you listen to the cut of that game, you will hear Jim Heavner starting to say, "Oh, Dean . . ." I didn't intentionally cut him off, but it worked out well.

There's no question that is the call I've heard the most in my career. Sometimes, I'll see it on TV when it's used over NCAA highlights. I like that a lot.

{.chapter-label} **Chapter 7**

From Heroes to Friends

Winning a championship in New Orleans began Michael Jordan's journey from quiet Wilmington native to global superstar. He went beyond being a sports hero. It always felt like he was someone everyone wanted to be—not just kids who looked up to him because of what he could do with a basketball but also adults.

I could relate to people's feelings about Jordan. I felt the same way—in many ways, I still do—about Charlie "Choo Choo" Justice. I'd watched him as a child and was amazed by what he could do on a football field. When I was able to get to know him away from the field, it was a dream come true. He was truly a hero of mine.

In Charlie's era, many of the players had been in the military. I was with him once when he was interviewed. He was asked why players from his generation seemed to get a special level of respect from fans. His response rang true to me. "It was post–World War II," he said, "and a lot of us were older. Coming out of the war, the public was looking for a hero-type individual, and sports filled some of those needs." It definitely was the age of the hero in America. In athletics, it was the same way. What set Charlie apart was that it wasn't just the public who loved him. His teammates felt the same way.

I've never seen one person capture the love of his teammates the way Charlie Justice did. You can tell a lot about a player by how his teammates feel about him. Justice came from a football era at Carolina when many of his teammates went on to great prominence in the real world. Paul Rizzo was an influential executive with IBM and served as the dean of the UNC business school. Art Weiner was vice president at Burlington Industries. Joe Neikirk was an executive with Norfolk Southern Railway. Among the players from that era were future lawyers and teachers and coaches and bankers and even a nuclear physicist, Ed Bilpuch. No matter what they went on to do, they all had one thing in common: they respected Charlie Justice.

The fans felt the same way. In 1949, Carolina played at LSU in a night game. Justice had such a reputation that LSU watered the field the night before just to try and slow him down. The Tigers wore white jerseys, and the game was played with a white football with black stripes on it. To those of us who were listening at home, it felt like big, bad LSU was doing everything possible within the rules—and maybe a few things a little bit outside of the rules—just to keep up with our Carolina boys. LSU won 13–7, but that's the only time my father and I ever went to the airport to welcome the team home. My father was upset Carolina lost the game, but he was even more upset about the way the Tar Heels were treated. We drove from Mebane to the Raleigh-Durham airport to be there when they arrived. Back then, the airport was just one building with a control tower. We had to park on the side of the road that led to the airport. We were two of many people who came out to greet the team.

I've never been around anyone since then who inspired that kind of affection. And the way Charlie Justice handled it made people like him even more. Anytime he spoke in public, he always mentioned his teammates. He would make these spectacular runs—people joked that he would run 50 yards because of all the side-to-side cuts just to gain five— and then spend his interviews crediting his blockers. He was unusual in a very, very positive way. He acted the way you'd hope an All-American would, though they often don't.

That was the Charlie Justice I knew as a boy and as a Carolina fan. To be able to work with my idol two decades later on the radio was beyond my wildest dreams.

I had several different color analysts in my early years doing Carolina football play-by-play. One season, we even rotated the analyst during the year. Gayle Bomar, Danny Talbott, Art Weiner, and Charlie Justice were among the players who served as analyst for one or two games each. The next season, 1975, Charlie did the games full-time with me. It was nearly 30 years after he had played in Chapel Hill, so not all the current players were aware of what he had accomplished.

We went with the team to play at Tulane and were watching the Tar Heels' walk-through at the Superdome on Friday night. A writer from the *Times-Picayune* was also there. He said, "By the way, whatever happened to Charlie Justice?"

And someone in the traveling party told him, "Walk right down there and ask him."

The next day, the *Times-Picayune* had a page-one column about Charlie Justice returning to Bourbon Street. The players on the team were overwhelmed that this guy they knew as a radio analyst was actually one of the greatest players in the history of the program.

I told him he was the only analyst I'd ever worked with who had previously inspired me to stand in line to get his autograph. There were times I looked over and couldn't believe I was sitting next to Charlie Justice. He was a big star to everyone in the Carolina football world, but he never acted like it in the booth. He took his radio work seriously and wanted to improve. He would always ask me, "Was that okay?" after certain plays until he began to get comfortable. That helped nurture our friendship, because even though he was undoubtedly the expert in the football realm I could give him some advice in the radio world. I believe he would have been a fine broadcaster and could have done that job for many years.

He wouldn't necessarily cheer for the Tar Heels, but he would definitely get excited about the games. He'd try to coach the players from the booth, saying things like, "Well, he should have cut right there," or "He should have gone the other way."

On one occasion, Orville Campbell, the publisher of the weekly newspaper in Chapel Hill, told him, "Charlie, of course you can see which way he should have gone. You're up here in the booth with the best seat in the house. You have to remember what it was like when you were down there on the field and everyone was trying to hit you."

Charlie laughed and said that was true.

Having him around was an asset for Carolina football. Johnny Elam was a backup quarterback and the starting punter. In his first game punting, he wasn't consistent. On the radio, Charlie said, "He's got a bad drop. That's why he's not getting better punts."

When we came out of the press box at the end of the game, Johnny Elam's father was standing there waiting. He said he'd been listening to the game on the radio and wanted to know if Charlie could show Johnny how to improve his drop. Charlie was famous for his running, but he'd also averaged nearly 40 yards per punt in Chapel Hill. So Charlie showed Johnny Elam how to get a better drop, and he became a much more consistent punter.

He could have been around Carolina football for many years in a similar role and been a major asset. I don't think he ever could have been a coach. Sometimes, it was frustrating for him that what came so easy for him as a player wasn't as easy for less gifted players. I think that's almost always the case for talented players who try to transition to coaching. But he could have been a tremendous ambassador for the program.

Unfortunately, that's not the way it happened. In the early 1970s, we didn't have much radio coverage in the Charlotte area. But Jim Heavner had a contact at WBT, and that's how he first obtained the radio rights. He could bring a bigger signal to the Charlotte area, and Dean Smith especially was excited about that. The down side was that the executives at WBT didn't like Charlie's voice. They thought it was too high and didn't fit his image. Sure, it was a little bit high. But he was doing well making the transition to being a broadcaster and would have done well. He was disappointed in the decisions made by Heavner and the WBT executives to remove him from the booth.

Woody with two of his childhood heroes, Art Weiner and Charlie Justice.

Even without constant exposure on the radio network, he remained the standard by which players were judged by a generation of Carolina football fans. Any great tailback who came into the program was hyped as "the next Charlie Justice." Of course, none of them ever was, just like no one was ever the next Phil Ford or the next James Worthy. That type of talent and personality comes along only once. Today, as we get farther from his career, and as the people who remember that career get older, I think his status has diminished a little, which saddens me. We even had a head coach who didn't understand why we had a statue of Charlie Justice. If people will read a little history and understand that the program existed before them, it will become obvious why his is the only statue outside the Kenan Football Center.

One of the greatest honors of my life was being asked to speak at Charlie's funeral. He was in every way the real thing.

If Charlie was my hero on the football side, the 1957 team was the same on the basketball side. I look back on it now and can't believe it—I called Charlie Justice a friend for many years, and I can say the same thing about many members of that undefeated national championship team. Young Woody Durham never would have believed it!

I see many similarities in the way the players on the '57 team interact with each other that remind me of how the Justice-era teammates related to each other. The '57 team jokes a lot but has a constant understanding of one fact: Lennie Rosenbluth was the man. Joe Quigg always laughs and says, "When we got in trouble, it never took very long. Coach McGuire would call a timeout, and he only had to say five words: 'Get the ball to Lennie.'" I've never sensed any resentment from Lennie's teammates about his status. They understood that to get where they wanted to go, they needed him to produce at a high level.

You want to know how good Lennie Rosenbluth was? Jackie Murdock played for Wake Forest in that era and hated Carolina about as much as anyone ever could. The rivalry between the two programs was intense in the late 1950s; it was that era's version of today's Carolina-Duke games.

But even with that level of passionate dislike for the Tar Heels, no one was a bigger advocate for getting Lennie into the North Carolina Sports Hall of Fame than Jackie Murdock. Lennie isn't always someone who wants to talk about his accomplishments. He's modest about them. People like Jackie and Lennie's teammates, though, aren't shy about speaking up to say how good he was.

The first time I had extended exposure to the 1957 team came when we did a fundraiser for the Wallace O'Neal Day School and four of the five starters came. Jean hit it off with Pat Rosenbluth, Lennie's wife, and we were already familiar with Joe and Carol Quigg. After that fundraiser, we kept in touch. Near the 50th anniversary of that team, the Rams Club did a fantastic event on the Outer Banks that included most of the starters, plus Eric Montross, Roy Williams, and Sylvia Hatchell. Over 800 people bought tickets.

Both in terms of social importance and on-court ability, I still believe that team deserves more credit than it gets. Many older Atlantic Coast Conference fans were introduced to college basketball by the 1957 North Carolina team. Before then, there wasn't a culture of college basketball in the Triangle area. It was important, sure, but nothing like it is today. The way that team captured the imagination of the state changed the way North Carolina felt about college basketball. Winning the national championship was significant. But watching a team do it in undefeated style, with a series of close finishes, hooked a generation of fans. The team had flair, in an era when bringing New York City style—which Frank McGuire and all his players possessed in abundance—to North Carolina was a big deal. Without the 1957 national champions, it's possible, and maybe even likely, that Carolina basketball as we know it would not exist today.

Only seven teams in the history of college basketball have finished the season as undefeated national champions: San Francisco in 1956; Carolina in 1957; UCLA in 1964, 1967, 1972, and 1973; and Indiana in 1976. That's quite a list. I'd like to see the Tar Heels from that era mentioned when Carolina fans discuss the greatest players in school history. Of course, players like Jordan and Worthy and Hansbrough will always be in that discussion. I think Rosenbluth should be, too. The prominent place he still holds in the record book tells you that, even though it was a different style of game, he dominated as much as players do today.

What a fortunate stroke it was for me to come along at a time when I could become friends with Charlie Justice and Lennie Rosenbluth, two of the most prominent names in the history of Carolina athletics. It's been a thrill.

Early in my career, it was easier to interact with the players because fewer restrictions were in place from the NCAA. There was a time, believe it or not, when we could have players over for dinner. Now, someone spends a night on a friend's couch and it's a three-game suspension. The relationships started to change in the early to mid-1980s. In many cases during the first decade or so I did Carolina games, even if I didn't get to know the players, I got to know their parents because they were always around. The Fords, the Worthys, the Jordans—all of them were tremendous people.

As for the coaches, each of them had his own personality and a different way to interact. Bill Dooley was the first coach I worked with, and I felt we had a good relationship. I tried hard to be close to his successor, Dick Crum, and it just never worked.

I got to know Mack Brown well. He chose to do his radio and television shows with the Village Companies rather than continuing with John Kilgo and Raycom, so that meant we spent more time together. I went out to Austin once after he left for Texas, and he and his wife, Sally, were extremely nice. I wouldn't say we kept in close contact after he moved to Texas, but when Jean and I saw Sally and him in New York in December of 2011, they were most gracious. Coach Brown always had a way of connecting with people.

Carl Torbush and I had an off-and-on relationship. I once misinterpreted something he said and wrote a column about it for Goheels.com. I had to hear through the grapevine—from three different people—that he was mad about it. I felt we had a strong enough relationship for him to talk to me about it himself without having to go through other people.

John Bunting was a different situation altogether. He was a great friend. We had not kept in close touch after he left Carolina, but from the moment he was named head coach we really connected. It was fun and nerve-racking at the same time because I wanted so much for him to succeed. But it wasn't working out because he didn't have the right people around him. He and I have talked about this. He needed a different set of assistants. He has said that he may have taken some bad advice on a couple of hires that turned out to be negative choices.

In terms of media approach, going from John Bunting to Butch Davis could not have been much more different. You always felt like Coach Bunting was your buddy. You never got that sense with Coach Davis. To get time with him, I went through his secretary or the sports information director, which I had never done before. What did help us connect, though, was that he liked to get things done quickly. I always felt he appreciated that I was prepared, and that he understood in most cases that I was trying to do a job. We did have a couple of situations when he didn't want specific questions to be asked. Sometimes, I could explain the goal of the question to him and he would be okay. Sometimes, he wouldn't.

On the basketball side, of course my longest relationship was with Coach Smith. Coach Guthridge was a completely different personality. I actually had a disagreement with him when he was an assistant coach.

I was at Durham Life Broadcasting and had a scheduled interview with Mike O'Koren. We were just making the changeover to videotape cameras, rather than film, and we had some camera issues. I called the basketball office to report we would be behind schedule. We were about 10 minutes late for the interview—and throughout my career, I made being on time, or early, a high priority.

The following weekend, Coach Smith said, "Coach Guthridge tells me you've been late for a lot of things."

I explained that I had been late for O'Koren because of a technical issue. It bothered me enough that I made an appointment with Coach Guthridge to discuss it. We ironed it out, and that completely changed our relationship. We became good friends. I'm proud to tell people that if they haven't had the treat of getting to know Bill Guthridge, they've missed a lot of what Carolina basketball is all about.

Some of the issues with Matt Doherty have been well chronicled. Perhaps even more so than Coach Davis, he wanted to do things his own way. On one occasion, I received an email that I felt fairly addressed something that had happened in a game, and I decided to show it to Coach Doherty. He read it, said, "Don't ever show me anything like this again," and balled it up and threw it in the trash can. In the end, little things like that were harmful to his career at Carolina. He was never on good terms with the maintenance staff at the Smith Center, and those were people he had to work with every single day. The head coach, for example, shouldn't be in a major shouting match over tickets. That's not something that needs to be his priority. I did later hear that Coach Doherty said, "If I had really thought it through and someone had advised me to do it, I would have kept Phil Ford on the staff." Who knows what difference that could have made? I don't think anyone thought to tell him that at the time. Everyone thought that since he played at Carolina, he would intuitively understand how issues like that should be handled.

My relationship with Roy Williams is most genuine. He has established a system that works, and he wants to follow that system. And when someone has won as many games as he has, there's no real reason to question it.

I was fortunate to work with so many different personalities on a close—and sometimes not so close—basis during my 40 years as the voice of the Tar Heels. Every single one of them made the job more interesting. Some of them even became good friends.

Memorable Moments

November 28, 1998 | Carolina 37, N.C. State 34 (OT)

"Davenport under center, pro I, ends in tight. Davenport back to throw, looking to his right, corner of the end zone, touchdown, Carolina! The Tar Heels win it! The Tar Heels win it!"

Getting into the formations evolved later in my career, especially as I was able to work with some talented analysts. It helped the listener visualize where the Tar Heels were on the field. I never wanted to get too heavily into the lingo because football coaches can use some words and phrases that don't make sense to those of us who don't live in their world.

From when I first started doing games, I was mindful of direction and color. I always gave the color of the jerseys at the beginning of the game, and sometimes I had an opportunity to work the color in again later. I specifically remember one game in the rain, and a Tar Heel wiped his muddy hands on his Carolina blue jersey. That's a vivid image for the listener.

Chapter 8

World Travels

Hanging just outside my at-home office door, I have two wall maps—one of the United States with 144 yellow pushpins in it and one of the world. Each pin represents a different location where I broadcast a Carolina football or basketball game. By the end of my 40 years, I'd traveled to 38 states and five foreign countries with the Tar Heels.

Until a few years ago, I had no idea how many places I'd been. Sitting with my sons, Wes and Taylor, one day, I said, "I'd like to have a map that would show all the places I've done games." I didn't have anything big in mind, but that Christmas they gave me the two maps. It's interesting to see how clustered together the pins are—I've never been to the Dakotas or Montana, for example. That northwestern part of the country just doesn't host too many games. I always joked with Wes that one of us would eventually go to a game in Boise, either to play Boise State or participate in the Humanitarian Bowl. Sure enough, one of us did—but it was Wes because Georgia Tech played in the bowl game. Contrary to what many people think about that area, he said he really enjoyed it.

I had an idea I'd been to a lot of places, but until I started looking back in the media guides at old schedules and putting in the pins, I had no idea how full that United States map would look.

Many of those pins came in the days when team travel was done on commercial airlines. The team would play a 9 P.M. game and then get up at 4 A.M. the next day to catch a flight so the players could attend 8 A.M. class. Charter air travel has meant dramatic changes for both teams and broadcasters. I was fortunate that our broadcast crew always traveled with the team because that is not true everywhere. Even when the basketball team sometimes took the smaller regional jets, it always found room for us. Don't think coaches fail to pay attention to the size of the airplane they use. On one occasion, we arrived at the Raleigh-Durham airport and saw Duke's plane waiting on the runway. We were in a smaller regional jet, and Duke was in a bigger aircraft. You can be sure the difference was noticed—and later brought up—by Roy Williams. Getting on those smaller planes is sometimes uncomfortable for normal-sized people, so you can imagine what it's like for a basketball team full of seven-footers.

Travel was not always fun. Some of the late nights and early wake-up calls could be a hassle. It was worth it, though, when the broadcast crew would get to be around the team in some unscripted settings. That's when we really got to know the coaches and players. When they were relaxed and talking to each other in a less formal setting, we got a window into their personalities. Fans see college basketball players on television every night and think of them as grown adults, but when you go to dinner with them and see what makes them laugh, you remember they're just college kids.

It never failed, though, that anytime we went out in public, we were treated with the utmost respect. At a restaurant like the Angus Barn or the Chop House, where the basketball team sometimes went for pre-trip meals before taking off from RDU for a road game, we'd walk through the regular dining room and hear the whispers right away: "There's Carolina." I don't believe I ever heard anything derogatory about the Tar Heels in those situations, even when fans of other teams were present.

It wasn't unusual in the days of commercial air travel for the team to be greeted over the PA microphone by the pilot. Of course, everyone on the plane had an idea they were sitting with some kind of basketball team—that many tall people didn't usually travel together. In most cases, the tallest players and the seniors would sit in first class, and the rest of the team would be in the back. Coach Smith didn't always come with us because he sometimes traveled on the day of the game. As someone once said, "He's a great believer in the philosophy that the general never travels with his troops." Naturally, if he was on the plane, almost everyone immediately recognized him and knew it was North Carolina. But if he wasn't with us, we'd hear a little buzz as people tried to figure out which team it was. Many times, the pilot would identify us and welcome the University of North Carolina. It never failed that the rest of the passengers would applaud. It was fun to see how much respect Carolina received all over the country.

You could even say the same thing for the rest of the world. My initial season doing the basketball games, 1971–72, was the first year the program went to Madrid, Spain. I didn't accompany the team on that trip but still had my usual television and radio obligations. This might seem like the Dark Ages now, but the broadcast crew had a difficult time getting a phone hookup with Coach Smith to record his audio over the game tape we'd acquired. It was the Christmas holidays, and many of the long-distance lines and transatlantic cables were tied up with people calling relatives. I couldn't get through to Coach Smith from the television studio, but I finally talked to him from my phone. The audio was not exactly pristine; I just held a recorder up to the phone while he talked.

Three years later, the Tar Heels went back to Spain, and this time I joined them. Talk about travel problems—that trip was one of the all-time hurdles. The night before the team left for Spain, it played a game at Yale. The next morning, we flew nonstop from Kennedy airport to Madrid. It was such a long flight that by the time we got there, Mitch Kupchak's back was in great pain, and he had to be carried off the plane.

The team practiced at the Real Madrid Sports Club. Jim Heavner was doing color with me, and we took our own engineer, Rick Edwards. While Rick was trying to set up during the Carolina practice, he was told we couldn't connect our equipment to the Real Madrid telephone lines because we supposedly owed another $500. That would have been a difficult situation even if we were communicating in English, but the other side didn't speak much English and we didn't speak much Spanish.

Jim came up with a solution to the problem: he decided to go interrupt Coach Smith during practice to tell him about the situation. I was still relatively new, but even if I'd been a 40-year veteran I still would have stood way back from that conversation. You simply didn't interrupt Coach Smith during practice, even on foreign soil. Coach Smith cut the discussion short and said, "Jim, I'll take care of that after practice is over."

Later that day, we had a meeting with the president of the Real Madrid Sports Club in a big boardroom at the downtown Madrid soccer stadium. We had a translator with us. It was obvious we spoke no Spanish, and we thought the people from the club spoke no English. The Real Madrid representatives kept telling Coach Smith the $500 fee was "in the yellow book."

Finally, Coach Smith said, "I want to see the yellow book."

They sent someone out to find it. At that point, it was less than 24 hours before the game, and we had no idea how we were going to get on the air. And if we did get on the air, we had no idea how much it was going to cost.

While the person sent after the yellow book was gone, a Real Madrid representative said to Coach Smith in perfect English, "Coach, would you consider coming back this summer for a basketball clinic?"

Coach Smith replied, "Let's talk about that after we see the yellow book."

Not surprisingly, the club waived the $500 fee. I remain certain that was because it wanted Coach Smith to return for the clinic. He was an important figure to European basketball coaches and fans. And by association, Carolina basketball was also important to them.

Of course, anytime you play in a foreign country, you never know what might happen with the officials. On that same trip to Spain, we played an exhibition game against a team from Cuba. The game was close. Walter Davis made a shot at the buzzer that was similar to the one at the end of regulation in the famous "eight points in 17 seconds" game against

Duke, except it was on the opposite side of the court. The shot would have won the game but was disallowed because it came after the buzzer. Our broadcast went to a commercial break after we told all the listeners the Tar Heels had lost.

But the drama was just beginning. The Cuban coach had basically bullied the officials into disallowing the basket. He even grabbed their whistles. As we went to commercial, we were marveling that he could get away with that. It turned out that he didn't. The FIBA representative went into the officials' locker room and locked the door. This was before video replay, so the only way to determine the validity of a last-second shot was to ask the referees. He asked them one question: "Was that shot good or not?" They replied that the shot was good. With that, the officials came back onto the court and signaled that the basket counted. The new final score was put on the scoreboard, and Carolina was the winner.

When we came back from commercial, we had to explain to some confused listeners what had happened: "When we went to break, we told you Carolina had lost. It turns out that the Tar Heels have won the game." I believe that's the only time I ever went to break believing I had seen one outcome, only to come back believing the opposite. The crowd loved it. When Carolina entered the gym the next night to play the championship game against Real Madrid, everyone in the building started chanting, "Da-vis! Da-vis!" with that Spanish accent. However, when a call in the game's early minutes went against Real Madrid, the eventual champion, the chants became, "Yankee, go home!"

Not everything went so well on that trip. We tried to locate a videotape of Walter's shot to use on Coach Smith's television show. Because of the difference in European and American televisions, we needed the Spaniards to dub us a copy. After Carolina lost to Real Madrid in the finals, I was trying to find the videotape and was walking down concrete steps in the arena. I missed a step, fell, and landed on my elbow. As soon as I arrived in the locker room, I told John Lacey, the trainer, "I took a bad fall, and I'm really hurting."

In those days, trainers tried to solve most anything with spray. That's what he did for me. He shot that spray on my elbow, and I went back to the team's hotel. At dinner that night, my elbow was still hurting, but I planned to put some ice on it and figured it would feel better the next morning.

When I woke up and went to the sink to throw some water on my face, I couldn't even lift my arm all the way. The team flew home that day. Susie and Dick Cashwell tried to make me comfortable as we headed to Kennedy in New York. When we arrived, I called an orthopedic surgeon friend of mine in Greensboro, Dr. Sam Sue, a Wake Forest alumnus, who told me I could come by his house when I got back home. He checked me out and then said something you never want to hear a doctor say: "Let me fix you a drink." He knew right away because of my range of motion that my elbow was broken. We had to go to the hospital and have a cast made. It wasn't exactly the kind of injury that could be kept a secret. I even had to do the television show with my arm in a cast. Coach Smith made me tell all the viewers what had happened.

As it turned out, that trip to Spain was one of the most eventful—a buzzer-beating shot, international politics just to get on the air, and a major injury to a broadcaster—we ever had. It also was one of the first occasions I was away for Christmas. Under Roy Williams, the basketball program has made a habit of always being home for Christmas. It was different under Coach Smith. His divorce made his family life complicated. I've always believed he liked being on the road at Christmas for that reason.

Being in Chapel Hill for Christmas wasn't always bad for him, however. Early in my Carolina career, we were working on the television show when he told me he'd been at his home in the Morgan Creek neighborhood on Christmas Eve. He heard carolers singing Christmas carols and thought about trying to pretend he wasn't home. He wanted nothing to do with the carolers. But he couldn't get the lights turned off fast enough, so he had to go to the door to see them—and there were James Taylor, Carly Simon, and a bunch of their neighbors. James Taylor's father was the dean of Carolina's medical school, and James and Carly had been married for less than a year at that point. Even Coach Smith saw the humor in that situation. He had frantically tried to get away from two of the most famous singers in America.

He understood that taking the players away from home could be tough for them. The most homesick I've ever seen a Carolina basketball team was on a trip to Tokyo. The crew had Christmas Day brunch with the players, and they were droopy. A friend of the program, Jack Petty, also happened to be one of my good friends. He never mentioned once to me that he had packed a Santa Claus suit in his bag. We were sitting at brunch when all of a sudden Jack showed up as Santa with individual bags of cookies for the players. The mood in that room made a complete turnaround.

One year, we were in Germany on Christmas. The team practiced on a military base. Coach Smith was very clear with the players. "I know you guys are missing being home on Christmas," he told them, "but we are bringing Christmas to these soldiers, and they're missing home, too." Coach Smith—who never let anyone unnecessary into practice—opened the gym to everyone who wanted to watch. When practice was over, he told the players, "We're going to stay until every autograph is signed and every picture is taken."

When you're that far from home and you see what a visit from Carolina basketball means to people, it really emphasizes that fans everywhere care very much about what might become routine for you. I think there was an understanding that Carolina basketball was a big deal in Chapel Hill and across North Carolina. But going to Madrid and England and Tokyo and many other places showed us that it wasn't just a local phenomenon. Carolina basketball was and is worldwide. It wasn't unusual to see a kid with a Carolina basketball T-shirt in the middle of a sumo wrestling palace in Tokyo. We went to the Canary Islands over Christmas in 1991, and the newspapers there covered the arrival of the North Carolina basketball team on the front page.

That Canary Islands trip was one of the great adventures I had with Mick Mixon. Because the trip was over Christmas, we stayed at home for a couple of days while the team went ahead. Through a series of flight cancellations and aircraft problems, it ended up that we weren't scheduled to land in the Canary Islands until three hours before tipoff, and our arrival location was 35 miles from the arena. Some of our broadcast team occasionally teased me about how early I liked to arrive at games. It wasn't

Roles reversed when Taylor interviewed Woody at halftime of the Carolina-Elon basketball game on December 29, 2011.
PHOTO BY MISSY DIKE

Woody with former broadcast partner Mick Mixon
Photo by Dan Sears, personal Collection

unusual for me to arrive three hours before kickoff or tipoff. That was because one year, the Duke radio crew had been caught in football traffic at Clemson and missed the entire first quarter of the game. I told Jean then, "As long as I'm doing the games, that will never happen to me."

Now, I was closer to it than ever. The arena in the Canary Islands wasn't modern. It was basically a community center. When Mick and I walked in, no one was in the building other than us. He was running all over the place trying to find phone lines we could use as a connection, and no one was there to tell us how we could get on the air. That's the closest we ever came to not broadcasting.

The trip got worse from there. After the game, Coach Smith invited us to ride the team bus back to the hotel, which was good because otherwise I guess we would've had to walk. On the bus, some of the players mentioned they thought there was a nude beach near the hotel. I felt like I had to check things out. Here's a lesson for you: before you visit a nude beach, find out if the main clientele is elderly people. I saw some things that day I'll never be able to forget.

Football bowl trips sometimes didn't present a problem at the holidays because for many years we didn't have the rights to broadcast postseason games. That probably sounds strange today, but when I started, companies like Westwood One and Mutual had exclusive radio contracts for bowl games. Jean and I watched the 1971 Gator Bowl from the stands with some friends. It wasn't until the 1992 season, when Mack Brown coached Carolina to the Peach Bowl, that our crew began regularly doing the bowl games.

It was an odd situation. We'd spend all season with the team, become invested in the wins and losses, and then we weren't there for the final game—a game that was supposed to be a reward for the players.

The most unusual bowl situation probably came in 1979. Going into the last two weeks of the season, it looked like the Tar Heels were going to be left out of the postseason. They were 5–3–1 with games left against Virginia and Duke. But a much smaller number of bowl games were played than is the case today. In those days, Dick Crum promised recruits that the team flew to all out-of-state games. We made the less-than-30-minute flight to Charlottesville, and as I was getting off the plane I asked Coach Crum, "Do we have any chance at a bowl game?"

He replied, "Woody, right now, we're not going anywhere. We haven't even been contacted by any game that is interested in having us."

It turned out to be a crazy game in Charlottesville. Matt Kupec was the quarterback, but the offense got bogged down and Crum substituted Chuck Sharp to run the option. Sharp helped Carolina win the game 13–7. Because of the results of some other games that day, it lined up that the Tar Heels could play Michigan in the Gator Bowl. Meanwhile, most of the players were going crazy after the win, but Kupec expressed some frustration to reporters about being taken out. At Coach Crum's press conference the following Tuesday, he made Kupec apologize for his behavior after the game. Plenty has been said and written about Dick Crum, but he did demand accountability, even from his star quarterback.

When Carolina played Michigan on December 28, the broadcast crew was in England on another basketball trip. Bob Holliday rigged up a way for us to listen with a telephone and a Marantz recorder. Just to pay the phone bill, it cost the eight of us who listened $40 apiece to hear the Gator Bowl.

That was cheap compared to the arrangements we had to make in 1983 to do the Peach Bowl against Florida State. The Peach Bowl was one of the rare bowl games that at the time would let the school networks cover the action. Carolina almost didn't go to the game because the Tar Heels had lost three of their last four games, and Crum let the players vote on accepting a bowl bid. Reportedly, they voted not to go. When he got the vote results, he said, "We need to vote again." And wouldn't you know it, when the players revoted, they chose to go to the game.

That was good news for our broadcast crew because we could do the game. The only problem was that the basketball team was in New York City for the ECAC Holiday Festival and would play St. John's on the evening of December 29. Jerry Richardson, who people now know as the owner of the Carolina Panthers, had once told me he would be willing to help if we ever got into a travel bind. This certainly qualified. He was gracious enough to come with his jet to pick us up in New York and fly us to Atlanta. It was around 12 degrees when we landed. Richardson took off his white New York Yankees sweater and handed it to me, saying, "You're going to need this tomorrow."

I still didn't realize how cold it was going to be. The radio booth was outdoors on the upper rim of the stadium. Midway through the first quarter, I reached for a cup of water and found it was frozen solid. Two things made it feel even colder. First, the scoreboard flashed that the temperature was minus eight degrees. That sounded about right. And second, Florida State smashed Carolina, winning 28–3. Coach Crum was so ticked that we didn't even get a postgame radio interview with him, even though his contract required him to do it. I came home on a commercial flight after the game. It wasn't until I was sitting in our den in front of a fire at around 9:30 or 10:00 P.M. that I finally got warm again.

Once we were able to regularly do the bowl games, we had some of our most memorable travel experiences. One of the closest calls came in December of 2004. Mick and I did the Continental Tire Bowl in Charlotte. James Spurling had arranged to have a state trooper pick us up in the tunnel of the football stadium as soon as the game ended. By law, the trooper wasn't allowed to turn on his lights, but we still made good time. We flew out of Concord rather than Charlotte because there was less commercial traffic. And we flew straight into Horace Williams Airport in Chapel Hill. We were in the car on the way to the Smith Center for the basketball game against Cleveland State when the pregame show went on the air. It was a little nerve-racking to be driving in the car and hear the Tar Heel Sports Network go on the air. That's not something I ever got used to.

Working for Carolina meant I had the luxury of doing games at three of the great venues in college sports: Kenan Stadium, Carmichael Auditorium, and the Dean Smith Center.

Coach Williams once told me that when he was at Kansas, he asked

Former athletic director John Swofford, Dean Smith, and Woody at the dedication of the Smith Center in January of 1986
PERSONAL COLLECTION

Max Falkenstein, the longtime Jayhawks radio man, if there was any venue where he wanted to do a game before he retired. That speaks to the kind of person Coach Williams is. He wanted Max to have an experience that was important to him. Max said, "I've never done a game at the Palestra in Philadelphia." Coach Williams picked up the phone, called Penn, and scheduled a game.

In the years before I retired, he asked me the same question. I gave it serious thought. Chicago Stadium, where the Bulls originally played, came to mind, but it closed in 1994 and was no longer a possibility. And I'd done a game at the United Center, where the Bulls play now. I'd been to the Palestra. I'd been to the Garden. I'd been to Pauley Pavilion at UCLA. I'd been to Hawaii and Alaska. The job had taken me to some great locations. I finally had to tell him, "Coach, as much as I appreciate it, I can't think of a single place I want to go that we haven't already been."

The first time I did a game at Madison Square Garden, I was so excited to be part of that building's history. Many fans, especially East Coast fans who understand the history of college basketball, think of that facility as the epicenter of the game. By the time I retired, doing games there had almost become routine. I knew what to expect—and most often, what to expect was that I had no idea what to expect. I had broadcast positions all over the Garden, from courtside to behind a television camera. Once, our crew was 14 stories above the playing floor. We interviewed Doug Moe at halftime of that game. He came up to our radio location, took one look at the view, and said, "You guys are missing a hell of a game."

On my last trip to the Garden, for the postseason NIT in 2010, someone in the travel party jokingly asked, "Are those elephants I smell?" He was not kidding; the place really did smell bad. It turned out there were actually elephants in the building. The circus was in town, and the animals were kept somewhere near the tunnel that led to the court.

Domes were always unique. On my first visit, I found the Superdome impressive. I did basketball and football games there. Carolina had some rich basketball history in that building. I did the basketball game against Texas at Cowboys Stadium in December of 2009. That's the kind of place where the venue rather than the game becomes the story.

Woody and Jean bundled up on the UNC basketball team's 1997 trip to Alaska.
PERSONAL COLLECTION

The polar opposite of the glitz of Cowboys Stadium came in the Orange Bowl Classic in December of 1985. Coach Smith took the team down there as a favor to Bill Foster, the former coach at Clemson. The team played at the Knight Convention Center. It was exactly what it sounds like—a convention center. The court was set up on an auditorium stage. The crowd was out in the auditorium, watching a basketball game taking place on a stage. That's how far Miami basketball has come. At that time, that was the best place the Hurricanes had to play.

In football, Michie Stadium at Army always ranks near the top of the lists of the best college football stadiums. Carolina played there in 1976, 1979, and 1991. I'll give Army fans credit for this: they are very into tailgating. As you arrive on campus, you immediately smell the food cooking and see the smoke coming off the grills. But as for the view, I don't remember too much about it. That's probably because by the time I got to our broadcast location, I was winded. There were no elevators to the press box, so we had to carry every bit of our radio equipment up the stairs—and it took a lot of radio equipment to get a game on the air. It made me want to load up a plate from some of those tailgaters and take it with me so I could have a reward after climbing those stairs.

On many occasions, those supposedly historic stadiums weren't quite what I expected. I had heard about the Orange Bowl all my life. That was one of those instances when "historic" actually meant "run-down." The Orange Bowl didn't even provide statistics in the radio booth. It's fairly standard anywhere in America that computer monitors provide updated stats. That's how the crew is able to tell you that Bryn Renner, for example, is six-for-nine for 72 yards passing. The Orange Bowl didn't have that feature. I asked a student assistant if we would be provided any kind of statistics. It took awhile for her to understand what I meant, though I can't imagine I was the first person to ask about it. After the first touchdown, I was brought a sheet ripped out of a pocket notebook. The sheet had the length of the drive written on it. That was the Orange Bowl's form of providing statistics.

That was also the year we arrived the same week as a hurricane. Not a Miami Hurricane, but a real hurricane. When we reached the

Miami airport on Friday afternoon, the bus took the team to have a walk-through at the stadium. The parking lot of the Orange Bowl was full of people who had lined up to get food, water, and hurricane relief. The next day, people were moved out of the upper deck because of worries about the security of the light towers. Meanwhile, there we sat in the press box on top of the upper deck. Welcome to the ACC.

Even a hurricane couldn't compare to the 1998 Las Vegas Bowl. People hear Las Vegas and think of the Strip. The stadium was nowhere near the Strip. You left the downtown area, drove straight down a road that looked like it was cut out of the desert, and arrived at what looked like a junior-college stadium.

Kickoff was in the early evening, and we arrived at 3:00 P.M. The weather was gorgeous—sunny and not too cold. At 3:30, the biggest sandstorm I have ever seen blew through. The wind remained constant throughout the game. I had done the pregame interview with Coach Carl Torbush at the team hotel that morning. As we got closer to kickoff, I realized that interview was totally worthless. I didn't mention the wind in that interview—because there was no wind at the time—and now it was going to be one of the major stories of the game. Carl was nice enough to redo the pregame interview with me. It was such a significant issue that when *Sports Illustrated* published its review of all the season's bowl games, its most outstanding player from the Las Vegas Bowl was Carolina punter Brian Schmitz because he'd punted so well despite the 45-miles-per-hour wind.

During the game, I hung my blue blazer on a hook at the back of our booth. When I went to get it afterward, it was almost brown because of all the sand that had blown into the booth. I didn't even wear it. I just threw it in with my dirty clothes and sent it to the cleaner.

Memorable Moments

January 27, 1993 | Carolina 82, Florida State 77

"Pressure by the Tar Heels in the backcourt with 1:50 to go. Sura hands it off to Ward, stolen by Lynch! Lynch will get the dunk as Carolina leads 78–77! The first time Carolina has led since it was five to two!"

That was one of the greatest comebacks in the history of the Smith Center. I relied on Mick Mixon, and later Jones Angell, to keep the running score of the game. During timeouts, when we had a break, I might ask off the air, "When was the last Carolina lead?" or something like that. I kept a notepad to the right of my score chart, and I'd jot down notes like that—last lead, biggest lead, biggest deficit—so I would have them in case they became relevant.

Chapter 9

Chapel Hill

I'd been doing the job for 13 years when we moved to Chapel Hill. We wanted to let Wes finish high school in Apex, and then we made the move from Cary in 1984.

There is something special about living in Chapel Hill. From my perspective, the biggest change was how much more accessible everything became. In basketball, I never had a regular schedule of which practices I wanted to attend, but I found it valuable every time I went. In football, my routine was to attend practice on Wednesday. I met with the coordinators each Thursday so I could have fresh questions from the previous day's practice. Those coordinator meetings were valuable because that's when they might give a heads-up if they were considering any different formations or personnel for the game that Saturday. When you're in the booth, the fewer unexpected things you encounter, the better broadcast you'll have. In that way, moving to Chapel Hill was a real bonus for my preparation, and therefore for the broadcasts.

When I moved to Chapel Hill, the radio network was owned by the Village Companies. I worked out of an office there. One day, Bob Woodruff came to meet with me. Early in the conversation, I could tell he was going to ask if I wanted to work out of my home. It took him a while to get to it, so I finally asked him, "Bob, are you here to ask if I want to work out of my home?" I told him I was willing to do that. I had a smaller space, but the upside was that it was always accessible to me at any time of day. And in the sports business, you get used to working some unusual hours.

Living in Chapel Hill enabled Jean and me to be part of one of the most unique college towns in America. The town and the university have a good relationship, but I don't think it's a feverish one. Dick Crum once made a very true statement: "Carolina wants to be Harvard or Yale during the week and Oklahoma on Saturday." That's a pretty good description.

When the Tar Heels went on the road to some venues, they would be packed before the teams ever ran out on the field or court. That doesn't happen at Carolina. The urgency to be there for every play of every game doesn't seem to be there. You can't blame all of that on the fans. You have to give them a reason to want to be there.

Traffic seems to be a big issue for Carolina fans. Sometimes when I talked about it, someone would reply that I didn't understand traffic because I didn't have to deal with it. That was true. I always stayed at least an hour after most fans left because I had to wrap up the show on the network. What I never understood was why people would go to a game when they knew they'd have to leave early. Why not give their tickets to Carolina fans who wanted to stay for the whole game? Some fans love to leave at the under-four-minute timeout in basketball. Why would they do that? Isn't winning the game the best part? When they leave early, they don't even get to see their team win the game. Don't get me started about leaving when the Tar Heels are behind. How many people will never forget that they left Carmichael Auditorium in March of 1974 convinced that Carolina had no chance at coming back against Duke? They missed the "eight points in 17 seconds" comeback, one of the all-time greatest in basketball history.

Roy Williams notices that kind of thing. He often references Kansas. His favorite story is the game when a big ice storm hit Lawrence. He even specifically told Wanda, his wife, "We're not going to have much of a crowd tonight." But when the team came out on the floor, Allen Field House was packed.

Wes did a Georgia Tech game at Kansas once when the Jackets had

KU down by 17 points. Kansas came back to win the game, and Wes called me later and said, "Tell Coach Williams I know what he is talking about. That's the most fan-involved arena I've ever seen."

Most games, you can predict beforehand what kind of crowd we'll have in Chapel Hill. In basketball, the Duke game is always electric. In football, before the Blue Zone was constructed, I developed a system: if I could look out of the radio booth and still see fans coming up the sidewalk between the old field house and the alumni center, I knew we'd have a good crowd.

When Butch Davis was fired, some people screamed that Carolina was de-emphasizing football. I don't believe that. But when you're in town, sometimes you do have to wonder how much passionate interest really exists in Carolina football. It's great that we have that history and that built-in infatuation with basketball. It very much highlights that the same intensity is not always present for football. In the old days, when the team still played the Blue-White basketball game, I remember many occasions when I watched our butts get kicked in football at Kenan Stadium, then walked over to Carmichael and found it already full with people excited about the basketball season. They had already made the transition from one to the other.

That's not to say I don't think Carolina can be successful in both football and basketball. It has happened here before. It always seems like as soon as Carolina gets a run going in football and big things are right around the corner, something happens to end the trend. I really hope Larry Fedora is the coach who can bring back that electric feeling on football Saturdays in Chapel Hill. When things are going well for Tar Heel athletics, the town feels completely different.

I've seen a lot of game-day changes since I became a Carolina fan. It used to be that people would park on the curb and any available square of grass. That created a certain community feeling. Now, you have to make a certain donation to the Rams Club to get a parking place. There's an incredible need for those donations, but that system also saps some of the spontaneity of game day. We don't make it quite as easy as it was in the past to be a Carolina football fan.

I love our band. I'd love to see it walk through Stadium Drive before a football game playing the fight song as loud as it can. I've even talked to the band director, Jeff Fuchs, about why the band members do so much of that jiving when they're walking to a game. He says he has to give them opportunities to do things they enjoy, rather than just the old standards. I believe the band plays an integral role in the college football atmosphere. I love those kids who participate in the band and think they do the best they can with what they are given. The problem is sometimes they're not given enough flexibility to create a fun environment. When Vince Carter was at Carolina, I told Jeff Fuchs there was an easy way to get the seats full before kickoff: allow Carter to be the drum major for one game. He'd done it in high school, and for better or worse, people would have shown up to see what he would do on a football field. But nothing ever came of it. When it comes to trying new things, Carolina almost always prefers to stick with what it's done in the past.

I've always supported going back to the "mike man"—someone like Greg Lunsford, who was the all-time best Carolina ever had at that job. Give the fans something that entertains them. When we couldn't find someone as good as Greg, we immediately gave up. Well, of course we couldn't find anyone as good. But did we give up basketball because we couldn't find another Dean Smith? It's not easy to grab a microphone and understand what's going to unite an entire student section. Greg had that gift. I believe some students came to games for the primary reason of seeing what he might do.

In fact, I believe he's the one who came up with the, "Woody, Woody, Woody!" chant. I don't remember the first time the fans did it. I had my headphones on, so I wouldn't always notice them. Someone would have to tap me on the shoulder and say, "They're calling you again." They'd keep chanting until I stood up so they could see me. I'd wave to them, and they'd all wave back. I used to tell everybody that chant was like Red Auerbach lighting his victory cigar in the Boston Garden. When the students felt comfortable enough to chant ol' Woody's name, that's when you knew Carolina had the game won.

You need those added attractions. You probably aren't going to find

60,000 people in Chapel Hill who want to come to a game solely to find out if you've improved your off-tackle running. You need some sideshows. Somewhere in the student body right now is someone who has a similar gift to Greg's. We'll never find him if we're not willing to look for him.

The best football game day I've ever seen was in Wisconsin. That university did a great job of bringing the crowd into the stadium and getting it involved with the band. At the end of the third quarter, the band played "Jump Around," and the entire stadium shook because the students were jumping up and down. It also played "Build Me Up Buttercup" during the game, and the entire stadium danced and sang along. When the game was over but we were still doing the postgame show in the radio booth, the band did what was called "the Fifth Quarter," which was essentially a full concert. The students stayed in their seats for the show and even sang along. By the time we made our way out an hour after the game, we passed about half a dozen open bars within a block of the stadium, and you couldn't have wedged one more person into any of them. That was a college football experience people wanted to be part of.

Notre Dame was on the other end of the spectrum but equally special. There were no fancy logos on the field. The team didn't even have its name or mascot in the end zone. There were no big video boards. Everything on game day was about only one thing: Notre Dame football. Notre Dame could do that because, much like Carolina basketball, everyone in the stadium understood the history and had a shared frame of reference that the program went beyond what happened on the field on any particular day.

Carolina football isn't quite to that level yet. You have to be a consistently good program, and you also have to reach the point that your fans expect you to be good—and those two things are not necessarily the same. When fans come to a game early in the season, you have to give them an experience that's positive enough that they'll be excited about coming back. That's how you build momentum.

We were almost there in Chapel Hill in 1996 and 1997. Mack Brown had built the program to the point that the only remaining steps were to win the conference, advance to a major bowl, and be in the discussion for

Woody with former Tar Heel football coach Mack Brown

PHOTO BY DAN SEARS, PERSONAL COLLECTION

a national title. Florida State was the major hurdle to all of those goals. Carolina hosted the Seminoles on November 8, 1997, and it was every bit as electric as what you would find today in Tuscaloosa or Baton Rouge. Students lined up for hours. Both teams were in the top five. ESPN was there. Kickoff was under the lights. On that night, fans saw what big-time football in Chapel Hill would be like.

Then the game started, and Florida State just kicked Carolina's butt. You could feel the crowd walking out of Kenan Stadium thinking, Same old, same old. It has been a challenge to overcome that feeling.

All of us who have been here a long time think we know the right way to "fix" Chapel Hill. We also have to acknowledge that it's still a special place. When people visit for the first or second time—or even the 100th time—there's something about the town that makes them want to stay. It seems like anyone who has ever attended Carolina wants to someday come back. Students don't want to leave when they graduate. It's a popular spot for retirees, but it's a great place for recent graduates, too. It's almost as if they understand the real world is out there but that as long as they keep one foot in Chapel Hill, they don't have to completely commit to entering it.

The town has changed. Franklin Street has changed. It doesn't serve the same purpose it did when I was in school, when none of us had cars and Franklin Street needed to be a place where students could walk to get everything they needed. My life as a student involved many nights of finishing work at WUNC around 6:00 or 6:30 and walking to the cafeteria on Franklin Street for dinner, or getting something I needed at Robbins Department Store. Imagine that—a department store on Franklin Street. Now, it's filled with T-shirt shops.

Franklin Street plays a different part for students now. On Friday and Saturday nights, sure, they need to be able to walk down there to see their friends. But on weekday afternoons, they hop in their cars and drive to Meadowmont or to the mall. Access to cars has changed the way the campus functions.

When visitors ask me what to see in Chapel Hill, I always tell them to park their cars and walk for a while. Most importantly, they should walk the campus. That's why people come here, and that's why they come back. They want to walk past the familiar buildings and see the spots that were important to them during what they remember as the best years of their lives. It doesn't matter what time of year it is—fall, winter, spring, summer—because there's something unique about campus in any season. I tell people to walk through campus and work up a good hunger, because no matter what they like they'll find something that meets their taste on Franklin Street. One of the biggest differences compared to when I was a student is that now it stretches all the way to Carrboro. If you stop before you go all the way there, you'll miss some of the best places on Franklin Street. Carrboro is a real place now, not just some little-known sidelight to Chapel Hill.

Any tour of Chapel Hill has to include some of the big sports locations. The basketball museum at the Smith Center is incredible. I'm hopeful that Coach Fedora will put some effort into bringing Kenan Stadium's Hall of Honor closer to what it used to be. I'd like fans to be able to walk in there—whether it's game day or any day—and get a real sense of the history of Carolina football. A famous Chapel Hill photographer named Bill Prouty used to make picture slides on the sideline during football games. That same day, if you walked down Franklin Street, you could see a rotating cycle of his pictures in the window of Foster's Camera Store. With all the technology we have, why couldn't we do something similar today and give people a reason to come to the Hall of Honor after a big win to relive some of the game's best moments?

Empty arenas fascinate me, so I always advise fans to try and walk through Kenan Stadium or the Smith Center. If they walk in there, they'll almost hear the crowd even if they're the only ones present. They'll be able to visualize what happened in their favorite game or when their favorite player had the ball.

The perfect Chapel Hill day always comes back to Franklin Street. It's such a touchstone for people that I've used it in several calls. Joe Quigg, who made the winning free throws in 1957, once told me, "As much as I enjoyed winning the national championship, one of the first things I thought when I got back to the hotel was, Boy, I would love to have been on Franklin Street."

In 1982, WRAL invited Joe and his wife, Carol, to come to Chapel

Hill from Fayetteville. They walked up Franklin Street before the national championship game. They had dinner in Chapel Hill and watched the game at Slugs, near Franklin Street. When the game was over, they returned to Franklin Street. Twenty-five years later, they got to see what it was really like on the night of a championship. Sure, the crowd was probably 10 times bigger in 1982. But it wasn't about the quantity of people there. It was about the feeling of being part of something like that. I run into just as many people who reference being present for memorable Franklin Street celebrations as I do people who went to the games that led to those parties. You can fit only so many people in an arena. Anyone can go to Franklin Street. You don't need a ticket or a parking pass. You just need to have a love for Carolina. That's what brings all those people together.

In 1993, our son Taylor went to Franklin Street when Carolina won the national championship. I have no idea what time he got home. A couple days later, Jean saw his shoes sitting in his room and said to me, "You need to see this. You're not going to believe it." There was still Carolina blue paint all over his sneakers, and the aroma coming off them was like nothing I'd ever smelled. None of us would have changed it for the world. That's part of Franklin Street, and that's why it will always be the core of Chapel Hill.

Memorable Moments

September 22, 2001 | Carolina 41, Florida State 9

"Here come the fans out onto the field. It is history! Carolina has scored its most impressive football victory, its biggest football win, since September of 1948. I mean the Tar Heels not only beat Florida State today, they hammered them."

Can you believe that in that game Carolina was down 9–7 at the half and won 41–9? I'll be honest, in the second half I thought we were going to score 50. That might have been the best performance by a John Bunting team. I know later on the Tar Heels beat Miami, but I thought that with what Florida State was doing at that particular time to everybody else, and the fact that we beat the Seminoles 41–9, that was unbelievable. We had lost consecutive games to Oklahoma, Maryland, and Texas. That's what made it so surprising. It was the most lopsided Florida State loss in 16 years.

The part about it being the biggest win since 1948, that wasn't something I looked up. I was always mindful of how the Charlie Justice team felt about its win in the opening game against Texas. Back then, college football polls did not come out until early October, which was probably more natural than what we have today. The players from the Justice era will tell you that if there had been a poll when they played Texas, it probably would have been a one-versus-two game. But people today aren't aware of it because it doesn't show up that way in our record books.

Chapter 10

Outside the Booth

The Rams Club started its spring tour as a way to take the head coaches into areas of the state that might not otherwise get to have much interaction with Carolina athletics. I served as the emcee for those events. While we went to the big towns—Raleigh, Charlotte, and the Triad area were three frequent stops—we also initially visited some of the smaller areas. It was interesting to watch how people in places like Lumberton, Laurinburg, Hickory, and Fayetteville took ownership of those meetings.

The idea was that people who might not get to interact with the head coaches on a regular basis would have the opportunity to hear them speak and feel more connection with the Tar Heels. In a way, I suppose it also helped people feel more of a connection with me. I didn't think of it as a chance to get my face out there, since I had been in television so long. But it never failed that at some of those meetings, a fan would approach me and say, "I'd know your voice anywhere. It's good to put a face with the voice." I still did the coaches' television shows long after I left regular TV work, but some Carolina fans thought of me as a radio voice, and this was their chance to see me in a different environment.

What I liked most about the Rams Club meetings was the opportunity for fans to see the coaches in different surroundings. It's one thing to see Dean Smith or Mack Brown on the sidelines. That's one side of their personalities. It's quite another to hear them answer questions from fans or talk with me about specific plays and games from the past season.

When we began taking the coaches around the state, there's no question about who was the most outstanding in those settings: Mack Brown. He could go to the podium in front of a room of 150 people, speak for 15 minutes, and have people thinking, Boy, I've spent all day looking forward to coming here tonight. Fans seemed to connect with his emotion. I believe they thought—and I also thought—it was genuine. He was—and is—an emotional person who invests a lot of himself in his teams. He cried on the air during our postgame interviews more than once. I specifically remember him struggling after a 17–16 loss to Wake Forest in 1989. That was the second of the back-to-back 1–10 seasons, and you just got the sense Carolina football was so close but wasn't quite there.

At the end of the first 1–10 season, the Tar Heels lost 35–29 at Duke. I remember saying to Coach Brown in the postgame show that he and the program were doing things off the field that made me believe he was going to be a successful coach. That wasn't necessarily a popular opinion. He lost 20 of his first 22 games in Chapel Hill. People asked me later, "What did you know that we didn't know?" The answer was two things. First, he was an effective recruiter. And second, part of the reason for that effectiveness was how quickly he was able to build relationships with people. That was obvious in a dinner setting like a Rams Club meeting. Every single person in that room left feeling they had a real personal connection with Mack Brown.

That doesn't mean fans had unlimited patience, though. Many people think the 31–24 win over Wake Forest in 1990 may have saved his job. The Tar Heels were coming off a heartbreaking home game against N.C. State, when they lost 12–9 on a 56-yard field goal. Wake Forest had been a thorn in Coach Brown's side, and to bounce back from the loss to State by beating the Deacons in Winston-Salem was an important win. Natrone Means scored the winning touchdown in that game.

That may have been the turning point. His third season, which ended

Woody interviewing Coach Mack Brown and Jason Stanicek on the day Stanicek broke UNC's record for total offense. The record was previously held by Charlie Justice, shown standing beside Woody.
PERSONAL COLLECTION

at 6–4–1, included a tie against the eventual national champion, Georgia Tech. In his fourth year, I thought the Tar Heels had a real chance at a postseason appearance, but they finished 7–4 and were shut out of a bowl game on the last day of the season. That was back when you could have a decent team and still not go to the postseason, unlike today.

Even with no bowls in his first four seasons, it was obvious people believed in Mack Brown. He had that gift. When the Rams Club started raising money for the Kenan Football Center in the mid-1990s, Coach Brown would have 10 or 12 potential donors out there with him every Wednesday when I would be at practice. They probably could have gone and stood in the huddle with the quarterback if they wanted to. After practice, he'd take them to dinner at the Carolina Club or have some sort of private catered dinner, and he'd explain the importance of the facility upgrades. He could really raise money. I think that's why his name comes up so often as a potential athletic director.

In the end, though, it was also money that disappointed me about the way he left Carolina for Texas. He made it about the money, which was what created some bitterness among Tar Heel fans. I believe that if he had stood up and said, "I've had a great 10 years here, and Sally and I have really enjoyed it. I hope Carolina fans understand this is an opportunity for me to go to one of the most renowned programs in the entire country," that would have made sense to me. Texas football is one of the top jobs in America. Johnny Harris was a big Carolina booster and a friend of Coach Brown. After Brown left for Texas, Johnny went out to see the facilities and told Mack, "You had to sleep on this a night before you made your decision?" That's how good a job it is at Texas. The coach there has absolutely everything he could ever want. And if he doesn't have it, the program will get it for him by tomorrow. That was the reason to take that job—not money.

The way Mack did it made Dick Baddour look worse than he should have. Carolina had never, ever paid a football coach the kind of money that was being talked about at Texas. (Incidentally, that's also why I don't think Mack will be an athletic director, because there is a sizable difference in the salaries of football coaches and athletic directors.) Mack

Brown makes $5 million per season right now. Carolina is paying Larry Fedora $1.7 million per season. Both those numbers are big figures, but the difference is a chasm.

It definitely ended poorly for Mack Brown at Carolina. That's a shame because he brought the football program to a place it hadn't been very often. Carolina was close to being one of those perennial powers that is in the discussion for big bowl bids every year. Prior to Mack Brown, the closest Carolina came to that in my tenure was 1980. That team was worthy of a bigger bowl game, but the loss at Oklahoma prevented it. The next season, a win over Clemson could have set up a memorable season. Instead, it ended in the Gator Bowl, and Dick Crum was never able to get the program back to that level.

That's the level Brown reached. He was one big win away from taking Carolina football to new heights. He drastically improved the talent level. He helped drastically improve the facilities. He had an uncanny nose for the type of improvements that would be important to recruits and help elevate the program.

It wasn't all perfect for Mack Brown, though. He hurt himself on the day Dean Smith retired because he complained that no writers were covering football practice. Well, Dean Smith's retirement was a national and maybe even worldwide story. Carolina's football practice was not a national story. That's something I'm sure he has never had to deal with at Texas.

I thought he had a chance to be the head coach at Carolina for a long time. I thought he was a great fit for the program. I gave him everything I could during those 1–10 seasons because I believed in what he was doing off the field. I even tried to find him someone to date when he and his wife got divorced. That's a relationship that goes beyond football coach and broadcaster.

You're never quite sure how much of that relationship is real. You spend almost every day of a football season with a coach because that's what is required for the job. You build a relationship. You're together in some good times and some bad times. Maybe that creates a false sense of close friendship.

I wrote Dick Crum a letter after he left Chapel Hill and never heard back from him. I never heard from Carl Torbush after he was fired. John Bunting and I have stayed in touch and even had dinner recently. I wrote Butch Davis a note on the day he was fired and never heard anything from him. I saw him three months later at the dedication of the Loudermilk Center, and all he said was, "How's your golf game?" That seemed awfully trivial to me, considering how much we had been through together. It was also surprising because, along with Mack Brown, Butch was one of the best at the Rams Club meetings. Coach Smith didn't like the meetings, which wasn't much of a secret. When he was there, he did a good job. But leading up to a meeting and after it, there was no question he would rather be doing something else. Butch had the ability to give you the idea there was nowhere else in the world he'd rather be than sitting with you at a Rams Club meeting.

Was that genuine? Well, it's probably not a coincidence that it was during his tenure that what used to be an extensive spring tour was trimmed back to five or six stops. That's not all Coach Davis's fault. Roy Williams also has a busy spring calendar, and it's tough for him to give a dozen different nights when he can travel across the state. The scheduling has flipped for those events. It used to be that the Rams Club planned the dates and put them on the calendars of the head coaches. Now, the coaches give the Rams Club a handful of dates, and the club plans the meetings around them.

One place you can be certain the tour will always stop is either Burlington or the Triad. For a long time, we went to Burlington every single year. That's not the biggest Rams Club chapter in the state, but it has Maurice Koury. I'll never forget one night we were at the Ramada Inn in Burlington, and it was packed. The chancellor was there, the athletic director was there, Dick Crum was there, and Dean Smith was there. Essentially, the entire athletic department was there. Coach Smith spoke last, as he usually did. He said, "I was looking down the table a few minutes ago, and I saw a lot of familiar faces. Chancellor Fordham is here. Coach Crum is here. John Swofford is here. What is everyone doing here? And then I thought, Oh, yes . . . Maurice."

The line got a big laugh because everyone knew it was true. Fans in the Carolina community may know Maurice's name, but I'm not sure they realize how much he does for the university as a whole. I'm amazed by his success story. His father and uncle had houses side by side. Between the two families, there were almost a dozen kids. They became so close that they were like brothers and sisters rather than cousins. They started making socks in the basement of their homes, and it grew into Carolina Hosiery. That's enabled him to be involved with real estate and other business activities.

People shortchange Maurice when they describe him as a "booster." To me, that implies someone who is interested only in athletics. If Maurice is a booster of anything, he's a booster of the entire University of North Carolina. The business school has the Koury Auditorium. A residence hall is named after him. Both the natatorium and a building at the dental school have his name on them. He's been one of the most generous people I know. I believe that although sometimes people are nervous about approaching him, he wants to be asked to participate in projects. I believe he truly wants to be involved. He may not give people exactly what they're asking for, but he's going to help them.

Coaches understand that. Everett Withers went to see Maurice the week after the win over Duke in the final game of the 2011 regular season. Butch Davis went and saw him after he was fired. It was the right thing to do. I've made my share of stops in Burlington. There are times Maurice asks questions people don't want to answer, but they are always informed questions that come from his passion for Carolina. He has always been extremely kind to me. He even introduced me when I was inducted into the Mebane Sports Hall of Fame.

One evening at a function, Joe Bray was shooting pictures. I asked him to take one of Maurice and me. I gave it to Milt Petty, who works with Maurice, and asked him if Maurice would sign it for me. Maurice never said anything about it, but Milt told me he was flattered to be asked. I've been fortunate enough to have a good relationship with him.

People who just interact with him at dinners or see him at games might think he's a fairly quiet person. It can be different in meetings when he makes his opinions known. At one point, Maurice owned University Mall and John Pope owned the Roses in the mall. Maurice wanted Roses out of there. I can't imagine what the meetings must have been like between those two strong-willed individuals as they tried to work out what would happen. Maurice Koury is not a man accustomed to letting someone else get his way.

The Rams Club meetings were a secondary aspect of the job. Calling games always came first. Once basketball season was over, I enjoyed the opportunity to get out and interact with Carolina fans at the meetings. I also felt it was important to connect with the Chapel Hill community away from Tar Heel sports. Dean Smith gave great advice to his players. He told them it was important that they should give to charity. But he also told them not to spread themselves too thin. Coach Smith's advice was to find one effort that you truly believed in and support it as much as you could. That didn't mean you contributed to only one cause in your entire life. It meant you found one group that touched you, and you help it all you could. That could be for a month or a year or many years. When you felt you'd run your course with that group, something else would come along that made sense as a great fit.

When I lived in Cary, I got involved with the Multiple Sclerosis Society. The society was able to put together a roast type of event that included Al McGuire, Billy Packer, and Dick Enberg. After two or three years, I was chairman of the Eastern North Carolina MS Society. I even went to the national convention in Houston, where I was able to meet Frank Sinatra, who at that time was very visible for the MS cause.

After we moved to Chapel Hill, I was approached by the Ronald McDonald House. The people there asked if I'd be the honorary chairperson of their fundraising drive. It seemed like a good cause. As I began working with them, they put me on the board of directors. One evening in 1988 at a board meeting, a friend of mine named Mike Haley said, "Let's do a golf tournament." He'd been the general chairman of the 1970 Greater Greensboro Open, so he knew some of the particulars. His idea was that

Woody and Dean Smith at the Carolina Kids Classic golf tournament. Woody is one of the founders of the event and Smith a longtime participant.
PERSONAL COLLECTION

he would be in charge of getting sponsors, and I'd be in charge of the golf. That became the Carolina Kids Classic. For the first five years, we raised money strictly for the Ronald McDonald House. Then we expanded to include the Childhood Trust and the North Carolina Children's Hospital. Carolina's coaches have been generous with their time for that event. Dean Smith still serves as the host emeritus. Most every year, the current head basketball and football coaches play golf and serve as honorary hosts. I'm proud to say we've raised over $3 million for children across North Carolina. Our next big project is a $7 million addition to the Ronald McDonald House.

As always, Jean is a big part of the support for that project. She may not get the attention she deserves because it's not a widely publicized event, but I can't count how many times she's been cooking a meal and has taken the time to make something extra to take by the Ronald McDonald House. She trained me well. Every time I was on a road trip with the football or basketball team, one of the first things I would do in the hotel was grab the shampoo and soap off the sink to bring home. After a few months, we'd collect all of it and take it over to the house, where it could be used by the guests. She also got involved with the UNC Lineberger Comprehensive Cancer Center and was instrumental in several of its Tickled Pink events. When I retired, I was approached about having a dinner at the Carolina Inn. I wasn't especially interested in that idea until I was told it was going to be a fundraiser for Lineberger. The event raised $25,000, which was fantastic. The center was nice enough to put our names on one of the consultation rooms in the hospital.

As Bubba Cunningham was getting comfortable in his new job as athletic director at Carolina, Rick Steinbacher, the associate A.D. for marketing, said to me, "Bubba is the best questioner and listener I've ever been around." Jean has that same ability. She is exactly the kind of volunteer every organization wants and needs. She always asks the right questions, and she thinks through all sides of an issue better than I do. She sees the positives and negatives and knows how to evaluate them. Sometimes, I get too emotional about issues. Jean can also be emotional, but it doesn't stop her from seeing the entire picture.

Memorable Moments

April 5, 1993 | Carolina 77, Michigan 71

"Michigan out of timeouts. Webber frontcourt, Carolina thought he traveled with it. Webber frontcourt, he takes a timeout—they're out of timeouts! Technical foul on Michigan! . . . The party is ready to begin on Franklin Street."

On the clip, Mick said, "Technical foul," right away. He was a stickler for the rules. Anytime we were in a situation where a detailed, specific rule had to be explained, I leaned on him. I know darn well that Coach Steve Fisher had told his players they didn't have any timeouts left. And even if Chris Webber hadn't called a timeout, he wasn't going to get out of a double-team between Derrick Phelps and George Lynch, two of Carolina's best defenders.

Webber did travel to start that play. I knew he traveled, and the Carolina bench knew he traveled because it went crazy. But I saw the play continuing, and obviously it was an important time in the game. So I knew I had to stay with the action and not get hung up on the missed call. I tried not to harp on calls by officials. And if there was ever a time not to do it, that was it. In a way, it's a lesson for young broadcasters, because if we had spent too much time on the missed call we would have missed the most important play of the game.

Chapter 11

The Family Business

I was in Spain with the basketball team when our younger son, Taylor, took his first steps. That was a part of the job that wasn't always fun. There were times, especially holidays, when I didn't get to decide for myself where I was going to be. I loved traveling with the team and being able to experience the way Carolina impacted people all over the world. But there's no one in the world who wouldn't exchange that for seeing his son take his first steps.

The flip side is that Wes and Taylor both were able to have some unique experiences because of my job. It may have shaped some of their career choices as they got older. Wes fell right into the sports world. He usually brought his basketball to games at Carmichael. While I was doing the postgame wrap-up, he would dribble up and down the court. By the time I signed off, he was red-faced and sweaty.

I tried my best to include my family in the games whenever I could. For the first six or eight years I did the games, I was fortunate enough to get two tickets near the top of Carmichael from the sports information office. I was thrilled just to have tickets. As I got closer to finishing my first decade of play-by-play, I finally worked up the courage to ask Coach

Smith for tickets out of the basketball office allotment. I knew exactly what he would say, but I was concerned about it appearing that I was trying to take advantage of my position. Coaches get endless requests for tickets, and I didn't want to be another name on that list. I didn't really feel like I had done anything to deserve tickets, to be honest with you.

If you know anything about Coach Smith, you can guess exactly what his response was: "Why didn't you ask me this before?" He put my tickets in the same area where all the basketball staff's family tickets were located. It was fantastic. Initially, we would get tickets for each game. Eventually, it progressed to the point that at the beginning of the year we received season tickets for that location.

When the team moved into the Smith Center, Jean had two tickets downstairs. She didn't particularly like it there. On a Rams Club trip in the off-season, Coach Smith asked me, "Do you think Jean would mind if we moved her upstairs?" He needed those downstairs seats for families of the players. I told him she would probably even enjoy that a little more. Soon after that, we began getting three tickets instead of two, so she could take a couple with her. Those seats in the "ring" of the Smith Center—the lowest four rows of the upper deck—are some of the best in the building. I watch games from there now also. We're in Section 212, Row C, and have a tremendous view of the floor.

Our kids got to attend games and knew I had a job with Carolina sports, but I'm not sure it was ever a big deal for them. They enjoyed their relationships with the players. They knew that sometimes when we were out to dinner or out in Chapel Hill, someone would approach us and say hello to me. Taylor called them "Woody sightings." When we were out and someone said, "Aren't you Woody Durham?" he said we had a "Woody sighting." In our neighborhood or among our kids' friends, I never got the sense that my job was talked about much or that anyone thought it was unique.

Whenever it was possible, I enjoyed being able to include my sons in certain games or special road trips. George Karl and Wes became buddies. When Wes turned seven, we had a birthday dinner for him at The Pines. It was before a 9 p.m. game, and George took the time to come by

Wes Durham with his father, Woody, at Kenan Stadium
PERSONAL COLLECTION

the restaurant and bring Wes a signed basketball. I don't know who was more excited, the adults who were at the dinner or Wes!

When he was just a little boy, Wes went with Jean and me to the Rainbow Classic in Hawaii. We were staying at the Waikiki Gateway with the team, and a big open-air bus pulled up in front of the hotel. Bobby Jones and George were sitting in the back. Everyone was headed to a team luau. All of a sudden, George said, "Hey, Wes, do you want to ride with us?" He didn't have to ask twice. Before I knew it, Wes had climbed up between Bobby and George.

During Wes's senior year at Elon, the Carolina basketball team went to England for an exhibition tournament at the Crystal Palace. As an early graduation present, he went with me. He was approximately the same age as the players, so when they went out at night, sometimes he would go with them. One afternoon, we were in Harrods department store when the warning bell went off for a bomb scare. At first, I thought maybe we had won a prize or that some item was about to be drastically reduced. Wes looked at me and said, "Dad, that's a warning for a bomb scare." You never knew what might happen on those international trips.

Taylor's big buddy was Al Wood. I'd come back with the team on a commercial flight, and sometimes Jean and Taylor would meet me at the airport. At one of those returns, Al picked Taylor up and put him on his shoulders. Taylor said, "Al, I watched last night. You had a pretty good game, but you did shoot a couple of bricks."

That became their big joke. One night when we were eating dinner at the Rathskeller, we saw Al, and he came over to our table to tell Taylor, "I haven't shot too many bricks lately."

In May of 2011, Al spoke at the Albemarle Hall of Fame dinner. As usual, he did a terrific job with his speech. As he was leaving, he tapped me on the shoulder and said, "Make sure you tell Taylor I haven't shot any bricks lately."

Wes and Taylor made lifelong memories hanging around with Carolina athletes.

Taylor's special trip was when the Tar Heels went to Orlando to play Stetson. A Carolina graduate named Bob Wacker who was high up in the

From left to right are Woody's son Wes, Wes's children Emily and Will, and Woody.
PERSONAL COLLECTION

Disney World hierarchy arranged for the team to get early entry before the gates opened to the public. For almost an hour, we had the run of the park all to ourselves.

I told Taylor I had to do some preparation and that we wouldn't have time to go out for dinner before the game. I gave him the room-service menu to pick out what he wanted, and he ordered prime rib. The next leg of that trip included a stop in Miami to play in a tournament. I was explaining that I'd need to do some more game preparation, but before I could even finish telling him the plan, he said, "I understand, Dad. Hey, can we get some more of that room service?" I guess life on the road with a basketball team wasn't all bad for a kid.

I didn't give much thought that either of the boys might want to follow their dad into the broadcasting business. The first inclination I had of their interest came from Wes. The summer before his junior year at Apex High School, he told me, "I've thought about this, and I think I'd like to do what you're doing."

He had always been around the broadcasts. When he was nine or 10, he worked as a gofer for me. When he wasn't running errands, he would sit in the back of the booth collecting scores. At that time, it required phone calls to press boxes around the country to get scores from the other games. On a couple of occasions, I heard him talking a lot, and I turned around and said, "What are you doing?"

He said, "Well, I called to get a score, and the guy from the other radio network asked if I could do a 30-second update on the game in Chapel Hill."

Even though he had that experience, I'd never considered broadcasting as a career for him. Once he said he was interested, I told him he had to build some practical experience. The next summer, he got a job in the promotions department of Capitol Broadcasting. He helped Capitol put on its big Fourth of July event at the North Carolina State Fairgrounds. I wanted Wes to get both promotions and sales experience because those are people you work with every day in the radio business. They are promoting and selling what you do during the broadcast. You have to understand how all sides of the business work in order to do the most effective job.

When Wes went to Elon, I got a call from Alan White, the athletic director, who had been an All-ACC defensive back at Wake Forest. He told me Elon was interested in having Wes work with its student radio station. For the first two years, Wes did color while a professor, Bob Anderson, did the play-by-play. For his final two years, Wes did play-by-play. That was great experience for him. He also interned at Channel 2 one summer because I wanted him to be exposed to television, in case he preferred that to radio. As it turned out, he didn't.

Despite all the experience he had, Wes got only two interviews when he graduated from Elon. It was a frustrating time for him. One of his applications went to Radford University. What he didn't know was that Oliver Purnell was the head basketball coach at Radford, and I had known him a little when he was an assistant to Lefty Driesell at Maryland. I called and said, "Oliver, Wes sent in his application. I'm not calling you because he's my son. I'm calling you because he can do the job. He's grown up around it, he had great experience in college, and he can handle it."

Oliver asked me to send him some cassettes as examples of Wes's work. In the meantime, though, Wes had received a letter from the Radford personnel office that indicated he was unqualified because of his lack of job experience. He was so down in the dumps I needed a spatula to get him off the floor.

A week or two later, we were sitting down for dinner and the phone rang. As usual when a college-aged kid is in the house, he was the first to answer. I heard Wes say, "Coach, how are you?"

It was Oliver Purnell, who told Wes he was about to go into a meeting about the broadcasting position. "I'm going to recommend you for the job," he said.

Wes looked a little confused. "Coach, I've already received a rejection letter from the personnel department."

Oliver said, "Wes, this is a basketball decision, not a personnel office decision."

Within a few days, Wes and one other candidate were invited to Radford for in-person interviews. Eight days later, he had the job.

He stayed at Radford for three years and was able to do basketball, Oliver's TV show, and some baseball games. From there, he moved to

Marshall, where Jim Donnan was the head football coach. Marshall was a good job, and I thought Wes might be there for four or five years.

The Tar Heels played at Rupp Arena in the 1992 NCAA regional. Cawood Ledford had just retired at Kentucky, and Charlie McAlexander, the Vanderbilt announcer, was taking the Kentucky job. Eddie Fogler was Vanderbilt's basketball coach and happened to be sitting next to Wes during Carolina's game against Ohio State in the regional. During a timeout, Eddie leaned over and said, "Wes, do you think you might be interested in our job?"

Five weeks later, Wes was on his way to Vanderbilt after just one year at Marshall.

Like Marshall, Vanderbilt was a good job. I didn't know how long he would be there. Three years later, Georgia Tech had a play-by-play opening. Wouldn't you know it? The athletic director who hired Wes for that job was Homer Rice, the same person who offered me my job at Carolina.

These days, it's fairly commonplace that someone will tell me how much alike Wes and I sound. But I never realized it until probably the end of his college career at Elon. I'd hear him answer the phone and say, "No, this isn't Woody. This is Wes." Sometimes, people would just start talking to him like he was me. I started to realize that we must sound pretty similar if people couldn't tell us apart on the telephone. It's been especially pronounced since he went to Georgia Tech. Occasionally, we've had friends visit Atlanta who'll tell me they were driving around in a rental car listening to the radio and wondering why Woody Durham was doing a Georgia Tech game. On one occasion after a Carolina–Georgia Tech game, I was in the car listening to the postgame show from WSB in Atlanta. The show played highlights from the game and ran my call and Wes's call back to back. Even Jean remarked on the similarity.

Fox Sports South once did a television feature on the two of us going head to head in the broadcast booth. That was the first time anyone made a big deal about our record against each other. At that point, I had an overall advantage in the number of wins for football and basketball. But Georgia Tech was starting to pick up some football wins, and Wes was closing in on me. The TV host found out I was keeping track of the head-to-head record. He told Wes, "Your dad says he's going to keep track as long as he has the lead." He was exactly right. When I lost the head-to-head lead during my last two years in the booth, I stopped keeping track. Carolina went through a stretch toward the end of my career when beating the Jackets in football was almost as tough as getting a football win at Virginia.

Wes made his broadcasting interest fairly obvious at a young age. I didn't realize Taylor had much interest until he went to Elon as a student. He was seven years younger than Wes. With his grades, he could have gone anywhere. When he chose not to go to Carolina, that was one of my first inklings that maybe he was trying to do something a little different than just going somewhere that he would be "Woody's son." What he didn't see coming—and what I didn't see coming either—is that at Elon, even with the age difference, he was "Wes's brother." For a variety of reasons, he didn't get the same opportunities Wes had to do some broadcasting in college. I'm also not sure Taylor had that same passion for it that Wes had.

When he graduated from Elon, Taylor went to work in sales for a station in South Carolina. That wasn't really what he wanted to do, so he moved to a company that had stations in Salisbury and Lexington, and from there to ISP in Winston-Salem. What's impressed me about how he's handled it is the amount of perseverance he's shown. He's kept hanging in there, and now he's doing play-by-play for Elon. In a way, it's like he's come full circle, because I believe he would've liked to do that job in college. He has play-by-play in basketball all to himself. My impression is that he's as happy as he has ever been. He loves Elon and the people there, and I can see that being a great fit for him for a long time.

By the way, Jean and I have only two sons, not three. At one point, I had several people come up to me and say, "I met your son Trip at Elon." I was surprised to hear that, since I don't have a son named Trip. It turned out that there was a student at Elon named Trip Durham. And because a couple other Durhams had been through school there, people assumed he was the next in line. He didn't correct anyone and let them believe he was my son.

Woody and his son Taylor on a golf trip to Ireland in 2000

And do you know where he works now? He's the PA announcer at Cameron Indoor Stadium. Now, we know for sure he's not my son.

One big advantage our family had in the business was that we could lean on each other for advice. Taylor and Wes always chided me about the fact that I did everything by hand. They told me I could save time and effort by doing things like my spotter boards on the computer. That might be true. But for some reason, when I wrote rather than typed, I remembered more effectively. The truth is, too, that I wasn't technically savvy enough to figure out how to do what I needed on the computer.

Other than their computer skills, we've shared many tips. Wes, for example, might call and ask how I put together my football drive chart. I'd explain how I took a big index card, broke it off into four quadrants—one for each quarter—and used the commercial breaks to fill in each drive. That made it much easier to recap the game quickly for the audience.

Even with our family connection, I don't believe we ever specifically discussed the idea of one of my sons following me in the Carolina broadcast booth. We were all much more interested in seeing them pursue their own careers.

Wes is in metropolitan Atlanta. That's a terrific place to be from a sports perspective. He's established himself as the voice of Georgia Tech and the voice of the Atlanta Falcons. Where else could he replicate that opportunity? At each of his stops, he's done a good job of not just listening to what my opinion might be, but of connecting with the important figures in that particular area. When he went to Vanderbilt, I advised him to contact John Ward, the voice of the Tennessee Volunteers. They became friends. At Georgia Tech, he became good friends with Larry Munson, the voice of the Georgia Bulldogs. Few people know there was a possibility that Wes could have succeeded Munson as the voice of the Bulldogs, which in the state of Georgia would have been quite a change. Can you imagine what it would be like if the Georgia Tech announcer switched to Georgia? There wouldn't be enough room on the Internet for all the comments.

During periods when he was frustrated with his situation at Georgia Tech, I think Wes might have considered coming to Chapel Hill. But he's so much more than "Woody's son" now. In some ways, it might have been a disservice to him. He's an important person in the radio business. He's friends with all the big names in the sports world, and he's building an influential radio show with Tony Barnhart. What Wes doesn't know about college football, Tony knows, and vice versa.

This is how far things have come. When Carolina was looking for a new football coach to replace Butch Davis, the university interviewed several candidates. The first person who told me the Tar Heels were going to hire Larry Fedora was Wes. He knew it before anyone else.

I'm happy my sons have followed me into the radio business. I'm even happier that they have made their own places in it.

Memorable Moments

October 9, 2004 | Carolina 30, N.C. State 24

"McLendon the tailback, Davis lines up under center. Thirty to 24, Carolina. Davis steps under center, will give the ball to McLendon. He leaps, he didn't get in! He fumbled the football! Carolina holds! The game is over!"

My call on this was tainted by the fact that T. A. McLendon was from Albemarle, and I had heard some stuff about him that wasn't uniformly positive. I didn't want a guy like that to beat us. From our broadcast booth, the end zone where the play took place was tough to see because of the angle. Until I saw the official coming in from the side, I wasn't entirely sure what the call might be.

October 30, 2004 | Carolina 31, Miami 28

> *"Greg Warren snapping, Jared Hall holding. Connor Barth for the possible win . . . Snap, spot, kick away, high enough, long enough, it's good! It's good! Carolina has won the game on a 42-yard field goal by freshman Connor Barth! Good gosh, Gertie!"*

It just came out. Some of the things I've said on the air, I'm at a loss to tell you where they came from. That was an incredibly tense moment, at least in the press box. I remember John Bunting telling me later that he tried to say something funny to Connor Barth to keep him loose before the kick. Connor said, "Coach, don't worry. I've got it."

The aftermath of that game was almost like Carolina had won a national championship. Flash attachments were going off all over, and the students were flooding the field. They got on the field so fast that Coach Bunting ended up pressed against the sideline reporter from the television network. He was telling me about it later, and I said, "Coach, she was fairly attractive."

And he just gave me that look and said, "Yes, she was."

There were probably some dead spots in that broadcast, but at some points I found myself just standing there watching what was going on down on the field. There had been few moments like that in that stadium. You have to have a feel for when silence speaks the loudest.

At Kenan Stadium, because of the backdrop, most of the time I had to wait until the official made his signal to call a kick good or no good. On this field goal, I knew it was going to be dramatic, make or miss.

Chapter 12

Transitions

The 1996–97 basketball team almost gave you the idea that the players had a sense Coach Smith might be at the end of his career. As that season progressed, they seemed to play a little harder and a little tougher. They started 0–3 in the conference, which seems amazing when you consider some of the players on that team—Vince Carter, Antawn Jamison, Ademola Okulaja, and Shammond Williams. That type of veteran talent was what enabled the Tar Heels to bounce back from the rough start and end the season winning the ACC Tournament and advancing to the Final Four.

Although he never used the word *retire*, I'd often heard Coach Smith say, "There are times I sometimes think I should step down." He said it after the 1996–97 season, but it didn't set off any warning bells for me. I thought it would be a similar case of taking some time off over the summer to recharge his batteries, just as he always had.

People often ask me if I had seen any signs that his retirement was coming. I saw none. In fact, I didn't even see any noticeable changes in his outlook or the way he ran the program. To me, the more noticeable

One of Woody's favorite shots of Dean Smith
PERSONAL COLLECTION

change came in the early 1990s. At that point in time, Duke was making a strong push. The Blue Devils started making regular Final Four appearances in the mid- to late 1980s, culminating in their back-to-back national titles in 1991 and 1992. As they excelled, there was some chatter among the fans that Coach Smith had lost touch with his program, and that maybe his recruiting was slipping. What did he do? He went out and recruited the class that included Eric Montross, Derrick Phelps, Brian Reese, and Pat Sullivan. It was almost like he heard the talk, too, and thought, *I'll show you guys*. People said he was slipping, so he went out and recruited the core of a national championship team.

He always did a terrific job of maintaining his role as the general of the program. Bill Guthridge was the colonel who took care of the details. The best example of that I ever saw came in Atlanta during the 1989 NCAA Tournament. Carolina was scheduled to play UCLA in a second-round game that was one of those contests the NCAA loves because it was a matchup of two of the marquee programs in college basketball in an elimination game. On Friday before the game was played on Sunday, J. R. Reid and Rodney Hyatt broke curfew. At that point, Reid was one of the biggest stars in college basketball. If he wasn't going to play against UCLA, it would be huge news. But at the Saturday press conference, Coach Smith never mentioned Reid was in trouble. The reason was simple: he didn't know yet.

Phil Ford made the bed check on Friday night and realized there was a problem with J. R. He took it to Coach Guthridge. As we were leaving the hotel for the press conference, Coach Guthridge said to Coach Smith, "We need to talk about something." Coach Smith asked to wait until after the news conference. It wasn't until he got to the locker room before practice that he found out about it. In true Coach Smith style, he turned the decision over to the seniors, Jeff Lebo and Steve Bucknall. Reid was close with Bucknall. But it was Steve who said, "Send him home." That's how Carolina basketball operated under Coach Smith. There were clear expectations, and everyone involved in the program understood they would face consequences when they weren't met.

That's how things ran with Coach Smith every day until his

Woody interviewing UNC basketball star Eric Montross, a future Tar Heel Sports Network broadcast partner

PHOTO BY HUGH MORTON, PERSONAL COLLECTION

retirement. Even in his last year, he put together a terrific team, winning big recruiting battles for Vince Carter and Antawn Jamison. College basketball was competitive enough that if he experienced a drop-off, you would have seen the evidence with recruiting first. And you don't assemble teams like the 1997 and 1998 Tar Heels without working as hard as possible on recruiting.

I was as surprised as everyone else when word began leaking out in October of 1997 that he was about to retire. His retirement announcement was the largest gathering I'd ever seen in Chapel Hill for a news conference. It was held in the old Bowles Hall, and it was packed. A host of former Carolina players were there, including Larry Brown, who was an NBA head coach at that time. I was also impressed that Georgetown coach John Thompson was there. People were aware of their relationship when they met in the 1982 championship game. They really did have a close friendship. Coach Thompson was complimentary of Coach Smith, and I knew it would be emotional for Coach Smith to see that his friend had made the effort to attend.

As that press conference unfolded, I felt almost a sense of disbelief. I had never worked with any other Carolina head basketball coach. I was fortunate enough to be with Coach Smith in pregame and postgame on the radio and television for 26 of his 36 years. We'd met when he was an assistant coach and I was a student. Mick Mixon and I did the radio broadcast of the press conference. As we were on the air, it dawned on me that this really was the end of an era. There would be no more Dean Smith basketball teams at Carolina. That's not just a basketball change. That's a culture change. It was emotional. And as he talked, it became emotional for him, too, especially as he tried to talk about all of his players.

It almost didn't feel right to start thinking about what would come next. Carolina would have to hire another head basketball coach, and that didn't feel right. When you look back on it, it's easy to form an opinion about how it unfolded. Coach Smith had been in a significant face-off with Chancellor Michael Hooker over the successor to Athletic Director John Swofford. Chancellor Hooker wanted Matt Kupec, and Coach Smith wanted Dick Baddour. My understanding is that Coach Smith wrote letters to other Carolina head coaches expressing the belief that the athletic department shouldn't be put in the hands of a fundraiser. Coach Smith won that argument, and Dick Baddour did some fantastic things for the Carolina athletic department.

But the damage to the trust with Chancellor Hooker was done. I don't think Coach Smith wanted the chancellor to hire the next basketball coach. When you look at the timing, it was almost as if Coach Smith took it down to the last possible moment. In early October, what else could the university do but move Bill Guthridge into the head-coaching position? Think about how much Coach Smith planned out every aspect of his team. Practice was planned down to the minute. Every possible game situation was reviewed and practiced. He wouldn't have left on the spur of the moment without a pretty good idea of what would happen next.

Before Coach Smith's retirement, fans and media members loved to speculate about the possible identity of the next coach. Coach Guthridge's name was rarely spoken. Personally, I thought Roy Williams would come back whenever Coach Smith decided to step down. In the mid- to late 1990s, Roy was a familiar face around Chapel Hill. He'd come back to watch his daughter, Kimberly, perform with the dance team. He watched his son, Scott, play as a walk-on for the basketball team. There seemed to be an obvious tie there. In my mind, I knew he had done a great job at Kansas, and I understood he liked Kansas, but I didn't think that feeling equaled the passion he had for Carolina.

I'm honestly not sure that Bill Guthridge had a burning desire to be the head basketball coach at North Carolina. But he was so selfless that he understood the situation called for him to do it. During his three-year head-coaching career, we talked about the situation during an interview. "I never thought it would be like this," he told me. "I thought five or six years from now, Coach Smith and I would ride off into the sunset together."

Roy Williams had the best description of the difference between being a head coach and an assistant coach. As an assistant, you make suggestions. As the head coach, you have to make decisions. Members of the

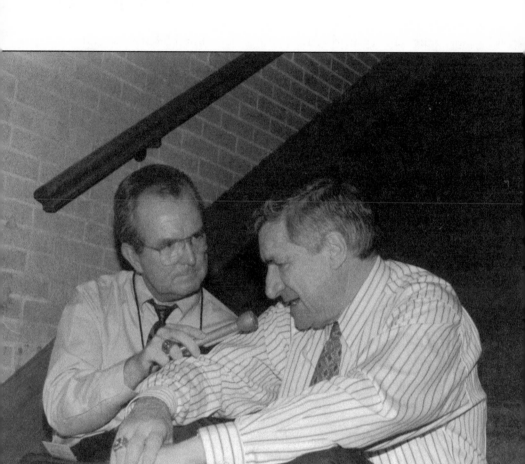

Woody interviewing Dean Smith in a stairwell at Cameron Indoor Stadium before a Carolina-Duke game
PERSONAL COLLECTION

public had a misconception of Coach Guthridge in that head-coaching role. They saw him as a mild-mannered guy sitting over on the bench who didn't have much to say. Maybe that's how it looked, but trust me, he could get mighty feisty when he was provoked. That was more obvious when he was an assistant coach. I remember an incident against Maryland when Lefty Driesell thought Phil Ford had fouled John Lucas. Lefty declined to shake Coach Smith's hand at the end of the game at Carmichael, and Coach Guthridge took major exception to that. What was so telling about the incident was that it wasn't that Lefty had done something specifically to Coach Guthridge. The snub was to Coach Smith, but Coach Guthridge wasn't going to let him get away with that. The two also had an incident at Cole Field House, and Coach Guthridge almost had to be picked up to get him away from Lefty. He and Lefty were jawing back and forth. At Maryland's old arena, the teams had to exit the court through the same tunnel, so there was no way to separate them.

Coach Guthridge had the unique ability to be a disciplinarian but also remain in touch with the players. He always had a good idea of whether it was time for a firm hand or a pat on the back. King Rice, who is now the head coach at Monmouth and played for Carolina from 1988 to 1991, told a story about Coach Guthridge during King's senior speech at the annual basketball banquet. "One day, I decided I was going to cut class," King said. "Later that day, I went to the basketball office and passed Coach Guthridge in the hall. He asked me, 'King, how was class today?' That gave me a very tough decision to make: was I going to lie to Coach Guthridge and risk getting in trouble for lying, or was I going to tell the truth and risk getting in trouble for telling the truth? I decided to tell the truth. 'I didn't go to class today, Coach,' I said. He looked back over his shoulder and shook his head a little bit and said, 'I know.' That was typical Coach Guthridge."

At the 2000 ACC Tournament, Carolina lost to Wake Forest in the quarterfinals and looked totally lost. Coach Guthridge kept the team in Charlotte and held practice the next day. At that practice, he lined the entire team up on the baseline and asked the Tar Heels if they were willing to make a commitment to play hard. What happened? They went all the way to the Final Four, which is where he ended his head-coaching career. He is one of the most unique individuals I've ever had the privilege to know during my association with Carolina. Anyone who hasn't had the chance to know him has missed a real gem. He deserves more credit than he gets for the success of the Tar Heel basketball program during his time on staff.

In my opinion, Coach Guthridge stepping down after the 1999–2000 season was also part of the plan. In a way, I believe he was falling on the sword. At that point, I think everyone thought Roy Williams was coming back to Carolina. That summer, we had the Carolina Kids Classic golf tournament. After the event, I met with a member of the Rams Club board of directors to discuss the tournament. During the course of that conversation, he said, "You know what's going to happen, don't you?" I didn't know. "Coach Guthridge is going to resign tomorrow," he said, "and Roy is coming back." He said it like it was a done deal. And in many people's minds, it probably was.

Jean and I left for Atlanta the next day. We watched the news conferences on television. At that time, Roy had not made his decision. Wes turned to me and said, "Dad, he isn't coming." I thought he was probably right. And once Roy came to Chapel Hill and then went back to Kansas without making a decision, I felt strongly that he probably was not coming to Carolina.

Once Roy made the choice to stay at Kansas, I wasn't sure what the next move would be. I never believed it would be Larry Brown. He had played at Carolina when I was an undergrad and was a heck of a basketball coach, but he didn't provide that feeling of permanence. He had a history of changing his mind quickly about jobs, and I didn't think that would be appealing to the people in charge of the athletic department. I thought it was a generous courtesy for Dick Baddour and Jack Evans to go to the West Coast to tell him he wasn't going to be the head coach, although he didn't see it that way.

I'll be honest: I thought it was going to work out when the coaching search landed on Matt Doherty. My thinking at the time was, *This is a guy who was on a national championship team. He's had a successful run as an as-*

sistant coach at Davidson and Kansas, so he understands what makes a good program. He knows how to make it work. Maybe I didn't put enough weight on the fact that he had been a head coach for only one season. Maybe that was more important than any of us realized. But when he started 21–2, he was almost a hero in Chapel Hill. What we know now that we didn't know then was that things had already begun to unravel for him. Some of the decisions he made with respect to his coaching staff and the office staff weren't well received, and that eventually hurt him.

He's told people I trust that he may have underestimated what a wide-ranging impact it would have when he let the incumbent staff go. I believe he thought there would be a trust that he would hire the right people, whether those people were Carolina alums or not. Look at what Roy Williams did—he brought in a staff that didn't have a single Carolina alum. He had many more Kansas connections on that staff than Carolina connections. Matt thought he was going to get that same leeway. What he didn't understand was that Roy had an established track record of running a successful program. He'd earned his leeway. Matt had one year as the head coach at Notre Dame. That wasn't enough to tell a proud program like North Carolina that he knew how to do things better than it did.

A question that came up frequently soon after Roy returned but has become less prevalent as time has passed concerned what would become of Phil Ford on the Carolina basketball staff. Coach Smith had been a good friend to Phil Ford. Phil is one of the most beloved players—if not *the* most beloved player—in Carolina basketball history. Beyond what Phil did for the Tar Heels as a player, he had become an important part of the program during his time as an assistant coach. I don't know that Phil could have saved Matt's coaching career at Carolina, but I know not having him didn't help Matt either. Roy was asked early after his return to Carolina about the future prospects for Phil Ford. He didn't say he wasn't going to hire him, but he didn't say he was, and I think that was painful for Phil.

With respect to both his assistant coach decisions and his overall program choices, Matt probably assumed he was going to have unconditional support. What he didn't understand was that he could make decisions or take actions that would begin to wear away that support. I believe he may have thought he could do anything he wanted and everyone would stay behind him. But no one—not even Dean Smith—had that kind of absolute freedom. Another factor in Matt's eroding support was his temper. He never personally showed me that white-hot temper that others saw. But he had vehement disagreements within the athletic department, sometimes over trivial issues. It's one thing to be passionate about important issues that are integral to the program. It's quite another to have silly blowups over things that shouldn't concern a head coach. I never specifically discussed any of the issues with the players. I didn't want to get into it with Matt either. But I could tell from the body language and demeanor of the players that things weren't going well. To me, that was the most telling thing.

Carolina basketball had been almost airtight under Dean Smith and Bill Guthridge. Little news trickled out of the locker room and reached the public. That began to change under Coach Doherty. And it felt like everything that was coming out was negative. This player was unhappy or those parents were concerned about the treatment of their son. Maybe that spoke to how smoothly things had run under the previous coaching staffs, because maybe no one ever became so upset that they felt they had no choice but to tell someone. As soon as one person is told something, they feel like they can tell one other person. Then that person tells someone, and before you know it word has spread faster than you could ever imagine. It's not wrong to say, "This is something we need to keep in-house."

In fact, Roy Williams has said that many times. Before the 2009 national championship game at Ford Field, I asked him during our pregame interview, "What keys to the game are you going to write on the chalkboard tonight?"

He said, "Woody, I don't tell anyone except the team that, so I'm not going to tell you that."

Would I like to have known the answer to that question? Of course. But I respected that even in today's era of information overload, some

Coach Dean Smith with Woody
PERSONAL COLLECTION

things are best kept within the team. He knew what Matt never seemed to figure out—that if you're successful, sooner or later those types of details will come out. And if you're not successful, maybe no one needed to know them anyway.

Team chemistry began to implode beginning with the loss at Clemson on February 18, 2001. The Tar Heels were sitting 21–2 at that point, but Matt had a shouting match with Joseph Forte at halftime of that game, and the team never recovered. In some ways, I'm not sure the entire Doherty regime ever recovered from that moment.

The next season was the 8–20 year, and we could all see it wasn't working. I felt the 8–20 season was even tougher than the back-to-back 1–10 football seasons under Mack Brown. During those football seasons, the games were difficult, but there was obvious evidence outside of game day that the program was moving in the right direction. It was exciting because I felt like I was watching the foundation of something special being built—and that's exactly what happened.

During the 8–20 basketball season, there was no foundation. It was one disaster after another, whether it was getting blown out in a game or opening the newspaper to find another unhappy player or parent. It was a major struggle, and I hated it for Matt. He'd been a player during a time when it was still possible to get to know players and their families. His mom and dad spent basically every February living at a local hotel, and Jean and I sometimes went to dinner with them. That meant he was more than just a head coach to me. He was someone whose family I knew and someone whose background I understood. Nobody pulled harder for him than I did, and nobody outside his family wanted him to succeed more than I did. But it was obvious even before his third season that it wasn't working.

Still, there was the promise of a great recruiting class coming in, led by Raymond Felton, Sean May, and Rashad McCants. All of us—right down to Carolina fans across the country and the state—wanted to believe that an injection of talent would solve the problems we had seen in 2001 and 2002. In hindsight, it might have been better to end the relationship with Matt after the 2001–2 season. Of course, you can also look back and say that maybe Roy Williams wouldn't have come back in 2002, and it ended up working out even though the program endured another year of struggle.

It was obvious when the 2002–03 team didn't win enough games to get into the NCAA Tournament that a change had to be made. It felt like the atmosphere around the basketball program had turned into a sense of relief when the season was over. That's not how basketball is supposed to be in Chapel Hill.

After that season, it turned into a circus for a week. I was concerned when some parents of players wanted to meet with the athletic department staff. I'm a parent. I know that when it comes to my children, I see everything through the viewpoint of what it means for them personally. It's risky to ask someone who feels that way for their opinion on how you should be running your basketball program. But I thought it was a good idea to talk to the players. They were in the locker room every day and had experienced every second of that season.

In hindsight, that was a week of struggles for Carolina basketball. Players and parents were trying to bring down a coach. And the coach maybe didn't have as much awareness as he should have about the problems within his program. The chancellor and athletic director probably could have phrased some things differently during the news conference. To top it off, the players at that news conference didn't represent Carolina the way people had come to expect. Fans were accustomed to seeing Carolina players in suits and ties at almost all public functions. But the press conference came together fairly quickly, and there was little time to communicate to the players that they would be attending with a crowd of media who would be eager to talk to them. They looked like typical college students, rather than the buttoned-down Tar Heels fans had come to expect. That was jarring for many people, especially when pictures of them were splashed across newspaper front pages the next day. The whole thing was almost surreal.

At the time Matt resigned—and he chose to resign, although everyone knew there was no way the situation could continue—Roy Williams was not the obvious choice. He had just turned down Carolina three years

Woody receiving the Atlantic Coast Conference's prestigious Skeeter Francis Award at the ACC Tournament in 2002
PERSONAL COLLECTION

prior. Many Carolina fans still had a bad taste in their mouths from the way that courtship ended. On the surface, it seemed like the Tar Heels would have to look somewhere else for a new head basketball coach. When fans asked me about the possibility of approaching Roy again, it almost felt like they thought it was just a courteous thing to do, but that there was no way he would actually come. He was one of the most successful college coaches in the country and had close Carolina ties. The call had to be made. But in those first moments after Matt left, I don't believe the majority of Carolina fans thought Roy Williams would be the next coach.

But the landscape had changed in Lawrence. Athletic Director Bob Frederick, a close friend of Coach Williams, had been reassigned to the school of education. The new athletic director fired Terry Allen, the head football coach, who was a close friend of Coach Williams. There is no question that Roy Williams was passionate about North Carolina. But without those moves within the Kansas athletic department, I'm not sure he would have come back to Chapel Hill. That's not a slight against him or his love for Carolina. It's a testament to what a great situation he had at Kansas. Even with all the changes he'd weathered, he still had a difficult time telling his players he was leaving. I don't believe he would have been willing to deal with those goodbyes if he hadn't felt somewhat betrayed by the leadership of the department.

Carolina was fortunate that things had deteriorated at Kansas. Have you ever thought about what would have happened if Roy Williams wasn't open to the possibility of coming back to Chapel Hill? Thank goodness Carolina never had to go there.

Memorable Moments

February 2, 1995 | Carolina 102, Duke 100 (2 OT)

"Gets it away to Donald Williams, down the side to Stackhouse. Stackhouse streaking in on Parks, reverse dunk is good, and he gets fouled by Parks! Oh, my goodness, what a dunk by Stackhouse. He jammed it on the reverse dunk."

A little bit later in that clip, Jerry Stackhouse came strutting out from under the basket, and I said, "It's the first time in his career I've ever seen him posture after a shot." Normally, he was all business. You might see only a little bit of a smile on his face, so it really caught my attention when he did it. And he should have, because it was a very impressive dunk.

Chapter 13

Football Gets Close

It's possible that none of us appreciated the stability we had at Carolina in the mid-1990s. Dean Smith was the basketball coach, Mack Brown was the football coach, and bowl games and NCAA Tournament appearances were commonplace.

It's just as possible that none of us anticipated the upheaval that followed the tenures of Coach Smith and Coach Brown. Coach Smith's retirement in October of 1997 began the most unsettled period I experienced during my 40 years as voice of the Tar Heels.

On the football side, Mack Brown had become an institution. The football team wasn't to the level of what Coach Smith had with basketball, but Mack had weathered those 1–10 years and made his program into one of the best in the Atlantic Coast Conference. He was a master recruiter. When you looked at a list of the top prospects in the state on signing day, most of them were headed to Chapel Hill. And when he supplemented that in-state talent with some quality players from surrounding areas like Virginia, the depth chart started to look much more promising.

Given his success as a recruiter, it's no stretch to say that his personality was magnetic. He could sell refrigerators to Eskimos. That was true whether he was raising money for the Kenan Football Center or sitting in the living room of a top high-school player. Raising money is the closest thing in college athletics to recruiting because you're selling yourself in both of them. He was also smart enough to surround himself with good people. Under Mack Brown, the Carolina football coaching staff was as good as it has ever been. He knew where his organization could be strengthened and understood how to find the right people to fill those roles.

By the time he left in 1997, Carolina had been to six straight bowl games. The Tar Heels had also played—and lost—two of the most significant contests of that era.

The one everyone remembers from 1996 is the 20–17 loss at Virginia, when a fourth-quarter Virginia interception that was returned for a touchdown completely changed the momentum of that game. In all likelihood, a win would have meant the Tar Heels would go to the Fiesta Bowl, which would have been a major step forward. They might have finished the season as a top-five team in the country and would have started the next year even higher than the preseason number-seven ranking they had in 1997.

Whenever anyone talks about the '96 loss at Virginia, they always say, "Well, if Mack hadn't called that pass play . . ." Mack didn't call that pass play. Offensive coordinator Greg Davis called it. Davis told me later that Carolina had run that particular pass play five times already in the game, and it had never failed to gain less than 10 yards. The truth was that the offense almost didn't have to score, since Brian Simmons had nearly returned his interception for a touchdown on the previous series. That would have given Carolina a 24–3 lead with 10 minutes left, and the game would essentially have been over. Instead, he was tackled in the red zone.

Greg told me he walked into the football offices on the Sunday following the game and apologized to Mack for making the wrong call in that situation. Mack said, "Were you trying to score?" Davis said he was, and Mack replied, "Then I've got no problem with it." That's the last time those two ever talked about it, and they've been together in coaching for many years.

The next summer, during the preseason ACC media tour, the intended receiver on the play, Octavus Barnes, provided another detail about what went wrong. Barnes said he had contact with a defensive back and stopped running. "Chris threw the ball to a spot, and I was supposed to be at that spot," Octavus said, talking about quarterback Chris Keldorf. "I didn't do what I was supposed to do." It goes to show that the snap judgment of what went wrong on any particular play in any game is almost always wrong. There are always many more details, many more variables that could have changed the outcome. What if Simmons got into the end zone? What if Barnes didn't get bumped? What if Davis played for a field goal instead of a touchdown? Who knows, but it's a safe guess that the next 15 years of Carolina football could have been very different.

Even after that excruciating loss, the 1997 team was still poised to make a major leap. The 1996 team was ahead of schedule. It had begun the season out of the top 25 and snuck up on some opponents. By 1997, it was different. Chris Keldorf wasn't taking anyone by surprise anymore, as he had done the previous year as a junior-college transfer. Everyone knew how good the defense with Simmons and Greg Ellis and Dré Bly was. The expectations were much higher, and that's why the Tar Heels began the season as a top-10 team.

Everyone was pointing at one game: the November 8 home contest with Florida State. That was the pinnacle of the Brown era. Both teams entered the game undefeated and in the national top five. All the ingredients were there. Kenan Stadium had as much electricity as I have ever seen, especially before the game. People talk about Carolina football fans as a late-arriving crowd. Trust me, no one arrived late for that one. It was a real window into how successful big-time football could be in Chapel Hill. It couldn't have been like that every Saturday because you don't play a top-five game most weeks. But Coach Brown had Carolina football at the point when you could expect to play in big-time games like that at least once per season.

Then the game started, and the air went out of that stadium about as fast as I had ever seen. Carolina was good that season. What people forget is that Florida State was really good, too. The Seminoles finished 11–1 and whipped Ohio State in the Sugar Bowl. Mack Brown had spent almost a decade telling people Carolina had to recruit speed. Florida State had been doing that at every single position since the 1980s. As soon as you watched the first couple series of that game, you understood that Carolina had some fast, talented players at several defensive positions. The Seminoles had them at every defensive position, and that's why they won 20–3.

Because things were going so well with the football program, it would have been natural for Mack to chafe at the attention given to the basketball program. Up until the day Coach Smith retired, I thought he handled the football-basketball relationship as well as any football coach I'd seen since I began doing play-by-play. He knew basketball had been good for him. When he was going through the 1–10 seasons, he was still able to get recruits on campus because they wanted to see Tar Heel basketball games.

It might sound easy for two successful coaches to coexist, but it's more difficult than fans might think. All coaches have egos. They want to be seen as the centerpiece of the athletic department. They want the best resources and the most coverage. And when Dean Smith and Carolina basketball were right down the street, it was always going to be a challenge for the football program to receive that kind of attention. But Mack Brown never gave me any indication that it bothered him until no reporters covered practice on the same day Coach Smith retired. That was my first indication that everything wasn't perfect.

I don't fault him for leaving for Texas. That's a marquee job. I do wish the departure had been handled differently. As the buzz was building about him being a candidate in Austin, he met with the players and told them, "Don't worry about me leaving." The next meeting he had with them, he told them he was leaving for Texas. That sudden change stunned some players and fans, and that's why his departure was so bitter.

Mack leaving for Texas set in motion a strange series of events that eventually led to Carl Torbush. He wasn't the first choice. Jim Donnan, who was then the coach at Georgia, looked like the most likely candidate. I happened to be at the Smith Center on the Sunday afternoon discussions were ongoing with Donnan. He would have been a big-name hire. He was coming off a 10–2 season at Georgia in 1997 after a successful coaching career at Marshall.

I still think Donnan may have wanted to take the Carolina job. Somehow, though, the communications got all confused. His side of the story was that he believed Carolina gave him a 5:00 P.M. deadline to decide whether he was taking the job. When I was at the Smith Center, I saw Steve Kirschner, the head of media relations, around 5:10. He was leaving Dick Baddour's office. He looked at me when we passed in the hall and mouthed, "He's not coming." That was the first time I knew that something had gone wrong.

Donnan later told a person close to the search on the Carolina side that the deadline really bothered him. He wasn't able to make a firm decision by 5 P.M., so he felt like he had to turn it down. It was so muddled that another meeting between the two sides was reportedly held the next day in Aiken, South Carolina, and he turned the job down again.

Now, Carolina was in a mess because it had deadlines on both sides. Because of the terrific play of the Tar Heel defense in 1997, Carl Torbush was one of the hottest assistant coaches in the country. Mack gave Dick Baddour a deadline: "If you don't make a decision about Carl as the head coach by 1 P.M., I'm going to take him with me to Texas as the defensive coordinator." Several players had also campaigned to Baddour for Torbush. It ended up that the program was basically pushed in Torbush's direction.

Carl was a good football coach as a defensive coordinator. He also had some talented players to work with, and coaches always say the right players make them look good. There was no question about whether he knew the game of football. What everyone missed, though, was that he didn't have any of the qualities that had helped Mack Brown get the program to its current status. He couldn't go into a high school, shake hands with a dozen people, and leave everyone feeling like they were his best friend.

He couldn't go into a room of donors and figure out exactly the right way to talk to them. I mean this in the best way possible, because this phrase also applies to some dear friends of mine, but Carl was a good old country boy. Getting people excited about football wasn't part of his makeup. It was like all the energy and excitement that had surrounded the program were instantly turned off. After winning the Gator Bowl, he lost his next three games as head coach. The program never regained any momentum. A 38–0 win over Duke at the end of his second season capped a 3–8 year and probably saved his job. The next season, even a 6–5 record wasn't enough for that.

When Torbush was coaching his last game and all the job speculation was swirling, I had given little thought to the name John Bunting. He wasn't one of the top candidates mentioned. When it got more serious with him, this is how crazy things were around the athletic department: I hoped we had found Matt Doherty part two. That was still considered a compliment in the fall and winter of 2000. Bunting was a Carolina guy and had found some success at the next level. He connected with the fans immediately. I'm not sure Carolina has ever had a football coach who the fan base has pulled for as hard as with John Bunting. He'd tease the fans a little bit, like with the win over Auburn in the Peach Bowl or the wins over Florida State and Miami. That was just enough to get them thinking anything was possible. And because he had the Carolina ties, that gave him a little extra credibility.

The fascinating aspect of the relationship between Bunting and the fan base was that he always seemed to earn the benefit of the doubt because of his Carolina ties. Matt Doherty had those same ties and almost never got the benefit of the doubt. In my opinion, that was because Matt expected it, whereas John worked at it.

I had a candid conversation with John Bunting near the end of the 2006 season. The school fired him in midseason, but he coached the remainder of the year. We were talking about his coaching staff, and I asked why he hadn't made some different hires. He told me he took some bad advice on his staff from Jim Webster. People thought those two were closely connected, but they actually hadn't been in touch much until they returned to Carolina. They did have a history together, though, and John listened to Webster's advice on certain coaches more than he should have. That really hurt him because he didn't have the staff around him that he needed to succeed in that situation.

I thought it was odd that John didn't have a better idea of the people he would want to hire to be on his coaching staff, and I asked him about it. He told me he had been so fully committed to professional football that he didn't have a good enough idea of the college football landscape. Even then, though, it was fairly commonplace for ex-NFL players to stop by practice when he was the head coach. I told him any of those players might have been a capable assistant coach. He said, "That's probably what I should have done."

In my opinion, John Bunting has done very well as an analyst. It's not an easy job. Some people throw around too many terms that the average fan doesn't know and make it too complicated. Some people don't know enough football. You have to find someone who strikes the right balance. In the games I've watched, John has been able to do that. If he chooses to pursue it, I think he has a bright future in the media.

The biggest challenge as a play-by-play man is developing a friendship with the head coach to the point that he feels he can trust you. Sometimes, that history with a coach can put an incident into an entirely different context. Consider these two incidents, which were almost 30 years apart.

In 1986, Eddie Fogler left his assistant-coaching position at Carolina for the head-coaching job at Wichita State. He had been a veteran on the staff. And although everyone knew Roy Williams was talented, the 1986 version of Roy was not the same as the 2012 version. John Lotz was doing some interviews for WCHL, and we were having an off-the-record conversation about recruiting. I made an offhand comment along the lines of, "I wish ol' Eddie was still here." It wasn't intended to be derogatory

From left to right are Woody, Buzz Peterson, Eddie Fogler, and Mick Mixon during the 1991 Final Four.
PHOTO BY HUGH MORTON, PERSONAL COLLECTION

toward anyone else, just complimentary to Eddie.

A few days later, I was in Coach Smith's office and he said, "I understand you were critical of Roy." I couldn't believe it. I explained what I had been trying to say. Coach Smith told me, "You probably need to talk to Roy."

I called him immediately. Roy said, "Woody, I understand. We've been friends for too long for something like that to change my opinion of you."

That's the kind of leeway you have with someone who knows you and knows the kind of work you've done. I was fortunate that Roy and I had a great relationship that enabled us to talk frankly when something needed to be clarified. The same was true with John Bunting and Bill Guthridge.

Contrast that to working with a relative Chapel Hill newcomer like Butch Davis. We didn't have that history together. At a charity event one spring, I made a joking comment about an assistant coach. It was a live auction, everyone was having fun, and I honestly meant no harm by it. I think that, over 40 years, I'd shown that I would never say anything in public with malice about any member of the Carolina athletic department.

That's not how it went over with Butch, though. By the next morning, our general manager, Gary Sobba, had already called me and told me I needed to go see Butch. I asked him how he knew that. He wouldn't tell me, which I thought was a little strange, considering that I worked for him.

Even though the comment was football related, I apologized to both Butch and Roy. I thought it was telling that when I met with Coach Williams, he said, "If you have a problem with Coach Davis, let me know." That tells you what kind of person he is. He understood that Butch might not have had all the information he needed about the situation, and that he was willing to intercede on my behalf if it was necessary.

It didn't turn out to be necessary, and Butch and I resolved everything. But it was nice to know I worked with understanding people who appreciated how I tried to conduct myself throughout my career.

Memorable Moments

January 2, 1993 | Carolina 21, Mississippi State 17

> *"It's blocked again! Picked up, it'll be a touchdown Carolina for Bracey Walker. He blocked his second punt and scores his second touchdown of the season. It's 14–13. Mr. Jordan, meet Mr. Walker!"*

Bracey had a knack for blocking kicks. You would have thought Mississippi State would be aware of him. The "Mr. Jordan, meet Mr. Walker" thing, it just came off the top of my head. It's not something that had been planned out.

Many times, people want to know where certain sayings come from. Chuck Thompson had a phrase, "Go to war, Miss Agnes." I was watching an NFL game when I was in high school. Johnny Unitas threw a long touchdown pass, and Raymond Berry pulled it in one-handed. The Memorial Stadium crowd was going so crazy that the camera platform was shaking. Chuck Thompson said, "Go to war, Miss Agnes," and I put it somewhere in the dim recesses of my mind, and sometime later in my career the saying just came out.

Chapter 14

Roy Williams Comes Home

In April of 2003, when Roy Williams took the head-coaching job, he went right back to work. People have a misperception that the summer is the off-season for college basketball. For players, that might be true. But for coaches, it's one of the busiest recruiting periods of the year. For that reason, I didn't immediately have the opportunity to spend significant time with him over those first few months. But I had a feeling he would be the same person I remembered from his previous stay in Chapel Hill. If you were his friend when he was selling calendars, you're his friend now. And by the same token, if you didn't have time for him when he was selling calendars, he probably doesn't have time for you now. He had a lot of history with many people in the area and is the type who doesn't forget those relationships.

When he was an assistant coach, Roy had a superstition that he had to have a candy bar in the pocket of his coat. In 1982, before Carolina played in the Final Four, he went to a convenience store across the street from the Superdome to make sure he had his candy bar. When Kansas played Duke in the 1991 national championship game in Indianapolis (Kansas had beaten Carolina in the Final Four), Jack Petty and I picked up a candy bar for Roy. I carried it as far as my media pass would let me, then passed it off to the security guard near the Jayhawks' locker room. Jack and I sat in the stands for that game. When Kansas walked out on the court, Jack stood up and patted the pocket of his jacket, and Roy looked at him and patted the pocket of his jacket, like he had it in there.

The main difference when he returned in 2003 was that I had primarily known him as an assistant coach, and now he was the boss. That's a different relationship. As I listened to his introductory press conference at the Smith Center, it was striking how confident he was. He had always been a confident person. But this was a different kind of confidence. He'd spent 15 years at Kansas and had learned what worked and what didn't. He wasn't a coach who was developing his style. He'd already developed it. And he was not the type to change something that worked. In 15 years, he had matured as a coach. He had supreme confidence that his style would work. Even on the sidelines during games, I've heard him tell his players, "Do what I tell you to do." It's that simple with him. If he tells you to run a play, run a play and it will work. If he tells you to go to class, go to class. If you're supposed to set a screen, set a screen.

Coach Smith had that same confidence but expressed it publicly in a different way. All successful coaches have egos. By the definition of their job, they're accustomed to being in charge. But Coach Smith wasn't opposed to letting people know he had to work to find the answers. In the winter of 1974–75, we were shooting his television show. Carolina was 5–3 and had lost consecutive games to Duke and N.C. State in the Big Four Tournament. In those days, the game films were actual film. When we finished the television show, he put the big canisters of film under his arm. As he was going out the door, he said, "Now, I have to go home and see if I can find a basketball team." Two months later, Carolina won the ACC Tournament. Phil Ford was the MVP of the tournament as a freshman. I'd say Coach Smith found a basketball team.

I was around Coach Smith frequently enough in pregame and postgame situations that I learned how to recognize when his wheels were turning. If Carolina lost a game or didn't play well in a win, I could watch him sit in that postgame interview and tell he was already thinking about

*Woody and wife Jean with Wanda and Roy Williams at a gala honoring Coach Williams in
Asheville in the spring of 2011*
PERSONAL COLLECTION

how to fix the issues he'd seen, even if no one else could see them. He could answer questions while thinking about something totally different. That's why sometimes his answers might not have seemed perfectly connected to the questions. It was because he wasn't really involved with the questions. He was involved with figuring out how to improve his team. It was pretty simple: if Coach Smith said he was going to fix something, it was going to get fixed. He was that good.

That's how you want to feel about your head coach. I was impressed with the way Roy quickly identified some problems with the program and some wounds and explained how he was going to fix them. A couple of his quotes reminded me of Coach Smith, particularly this one: "I don't want to take what the defense gives us. I want to take what I want." That was straight out of Coach Smith's philosophy. I was impressed with how he handled that first evening. I thought it was obvious that because he already knew a great deal about Matt Doherty from having worked with him at Kansas, Roy had a good idea of some of the issues he would need to solve. It wasn't like he showed up in Chapel Hill and had to start asking people what went wrong.

When he took the job, he'd brought Kansas to two straight Final Fours and the national championship game in 2003. There was no question about whether he could coach. The question was whether he could get the players who were already on the roster to play together. He is a coach who very much values recruiting the players who best fit his program. To be handed a fully intact roster stocked with players he had no relationship with was a bigger challenge than some people realize. Roy complimented Jackie Manuel several times in that first season and often commented that Jackie was the first player to fully commit to what the coaching staff asked him to do. You had to think about that comment from the other perspective also: what was he saying about the players who weren't Jackie Manuel? That was the biggest challenge with the 2003–4 team.

It wasn't that the team didn't have any talent. It was that it took an entire season for that group to fully trust what Roy Williams was saying and to get rid of the bad habits and attitudes that had developed over the previous seasons. While he had been winning 80 percent of his games at Kansas, the players Roy inherited had won 32 of their previous 73 games. That's pretty remarkable, especially knowing what we do now about how successful he was going to be at Carolina. Despite the numbers that were overwhelmingly in his favor, it took a whole year for players to buy in. That's why coaching isn't as easy as some people think it might be. You can be the greatest technical coach in the world and draw up the greatest plays, but if your players don't believe in you it's not going to work.

On the court, fans saw immediate parallels to the style favored by Dean Smith. Going inside was the primary option at all times. Coach Smith used to tell his teams that one pass should go inside before anything was attempted on the outside. That was a new idea for the 2003–04 team.

At his opening press conference, Roy told the players directly, "You are really going to be coached." That was an interesting comment. You never would have heard Dean Smith say that, but he didn't have to, because anyone who came to play for him would already know that. It might not have been so understood by Roy's players, who had developed some of their own ideas. Roy let them know on the very first night that things were changing.

It was remarkable how he turned a group that sometimes wasn't sold on him into the national champion in 2004–05. Some people said that a good coach couldn't become a great coach until he won a national championship, which was absurd. Roy Williams had been close to winning a national title at Kansas. Beating Illinois in St. Louis in 2005 didn't suddenly validate him as a coach. Anyone who knew anything about college basketball understood he was one of the game's elite coaches. But even if you know something isn't true, if you hear it over and over again it starts to make you wonder. As I saw Roy celebrate in 2005 and go into the stands to hug his family, it was pleasant to know he'd never have to hear the questions again.

Tyler Hansbrough was in the stands that night in St. Louis. At that point, I'm not sure I could have picked him out of the crowd. But it wasn't long before I started hearing a great deal about him during preseason practice. Coach Williams continued a tradition started by Coach Smith. All the coaches with Carolina ties were invited back to Chapel Hill for a weekend of basketball talks in the late summer. As Roy was describing his plans for his 2005–06 team at those talks, Jeff Lebo remembers thinking, You're putting a lot of eggs in the basket of some freshman named Tyler Hansbrough. But by the middle of Hansbrough's freshman season, Lebo called Roy and said, "Now, I see what you mean."

Credit Roy for realizing right away that Hansbrough was the kind of player around whom he could build a team. He understood immediately what Hansbrough was capable of doing and how that fit into the kind of game Carolina wanted to play. What always amazed me about Tyler was that he was a marked man so early in his career. Other teams had him on the scouting report quickly. Despite the fact that they were geared up to stop him, he delivered almost every time. I couldn't get over how consistent he was inside, even with teams sending two defenders at him and trying to push him around. If the Tar Heels could get the ball to him, something good was going to happen.

It was so enjoyable to watch Tyler's class—which also included Bobby Frasor, Danny Green, Marcus Ginyard, and Mike Copeland—go through its four-year progression. Their teams surprised everyone in 2006, came close to the Final Four in 2007, made it to the Final Four in 2008, and won it all in 2009. That's a prototype for a four-year college career.

The way the Tar Heels won it in 2009 was one of the most impressive performances I saw during my broadcasting career. You have to put the 2009 squad among the five best Carolina teams of all time because any team that wins an NCAA championship is special. I would put the 2009 team right there with the 1982 team. The games were closer for the 1982 team, but I always appreciated how that group seemed to have the perfect fit at every position, including the reserves, who understood what they were expected to do.

I knew the '09 team was good. I had no idea it was going to jump on Michigan State the way it did in the championship game in Detroit. That made it a different broadcast. Some people have said it was obvious the game was over at halftime. You never want to think that way, but it was clear that the Tar Heels were doing what they wanted to do, when they wanted to do it. There wasn't one single time that I got the feeling Michigan State was about to make a push, even with the help of a Detroit crowd that was pro-MSU.

It was one of the most unique championship games I ever called. It was rare to do a game at the Final Four when everyone wasn't on the edge of their seats. But everything that happened that night was positive for Carolina. It was obvious from the tipoff that Michigan State could not play to the level of the Tar Heels, and that Carolina was supremely ready to play. Before the game, I had wondered if some psychology might be in play because the Tar Heels had whipped Michigan State in that same arena earlier in the year. Sometimes, being the loser in that first game can help you in the second game. Indiana lost to Carolina during the 1980–81 regular season but beat the Tar Heels in the championship game. Carolina lost to Michigan during the 1992–93 regular season but beat the Wolverines in the championship game. I knew about that history and thought Michigan State might have the psychological edge. Maybe the Spartans did have the mental edge. But what everyone found out that night is that if you have the mental edge and we have Ty Lawson, Tyler Hansbrough, Wayne Ellington, and the rest of the 2009 roster, plus Roy Williams on the sidelines, we're going to beat you by 17 points and the game will never be close. It was a comfortable game to do.

Broadcasting games in the NCAA Tournament was always unique because it provided the opportunity to see radio crews we didn't normally see during a typical season. The Michigan State crew members were demonstrative. Our engineer, Ben Alexander, even mentioned it during one of the commercial breaks. They got excited when the Spartans scored and were obviously displeased by certain officiating calls.

It was unusual to see that kind of expressive behavior from a major-college radio crew. The first year Boston College was in the ACC, its crew was incredibly demonstrative. The broadcasters weren't just visible on press row, they also openly criticized the league officials and front office on the air and implied that the league was biased toward the teams from the state of North Carolina. It got to the point that the commissioner had to let the crew and the athletic director know that wasn't how we did things in the ACC.

Of course, every broadcaster has to say something about the officiating at some point. I know that Bob Harris at Duke has been asked several times to tone down his discussions of the referees. At one point, there was a cassette tape that contained all his criticisms of the officials, and it eventually found its way to the league office. It got to the point that I wish I would have pulled him aside or had lunch with him to talk about it.

I tried my best to stay away from talking about the referees. I believe it takes away from the quality of the broadcast. People aren't tuning in to hear about the officials. They are tuning in to hear about the players and coaches. Sometimes, broadcasters forget that referees are paid to know every detail of every rule. If you're going to get into a discussion of the officiating, you better be certain you're right and pick your spots because otherwise the audience will tune you out and say, "Oh, there he goes again." Anytime the audience tunes you out—for any reason—you're not doing your job as a broadcaster.

I did not see the 2009–10 season coming. I don't believe anyone did, and that's why it was such a difficult year for Roy Williams. It turned into the perfect storm of bad circumstances. There were personality issues on the roster, which was unusual for a Williams-coached team. Will Graves was dismissed before the season started. There was a series of injuries. The Wear brothers were a problem. I was never a fan of Larry Drew II's body language, either on the court or off it. The team just never came together.

With the games an almost constant struggle, the most memorable part of that season was the 100 years celebration. That was the latest example of Roy taking his job seriously. That very first night, he had said he wasn't coaching a team, he was coaching a program. The way he's integrated the history of Carolina basketball shows how serious he is about that part of his role. In the less than 10 years since he's returned, the Tar Heels have had ceremonies for all the lettermen, a reunion of the 1982 and 1957 teams, a reunion of the 1971 NIT champions, and the year-long centennial celebration. That's an effective way to remind everyone—both fans and players—that they're part of something bigger.

The first reunion, in 2004, was one of my favorite nongame memories as a broadcaster. Coach Williams challenged me: he told me that when Kansas had held a similar reunion, the Jayhawks introduced every single person by name. The organizers wanted to introduce all the Carolina lettermen in attendance at halftime of the game against Florida State. That meant we had to get everyone on the court, announce their names, and get them off the court before the teams came out to warm up. That wasn't an easy assignment with nearly 225 lettermen in attendance, which spoke to how strongly the alumni felt about Carolina basketball. When Roy gave them a reason to return and an opportunity to be part of the program again on that day, they responded in huge numbers.

I got through every single name at halftime. The first thing I did when I read the last name was look at the game clock. Three minutes were still left until halftime was over. I'd call that a success.

There was a brief moment when for some reason I was afraid I'd skipped Jeff Denny. When I saw him that night at the banquet, I said, "Jeff, I've been concerned that I missed you during the introductions."

He just laughed. "You called me," he said. "The players were all talking about how amazed we were that you got through everyone's name and finished it before halftime."

Sometimes, even old broadcasters can rise to the challenge.

Memorable Moments

April 4, 2005 | Carolina 75, Illinois 70

"Long outside shot is short. Rebounded May, it's over! Carolina has won the national championship!"

In 2005 in St. Louis, I felt the same way for Roy Williams that I felt for Coach Smith in 1982 in New Orleans. Roy was hearing some stuff from the national media about "winning the big one." I felt so good for him that night.

It's silly that after we spend an entire season with a team, the NCAA won't let us have the head coach on the air immediately after the game because he's sent straight to the television crew. Fortunately that night, Roy came over to me and we did a quick interview on the baseline. I also went up in the stands. His wife, Wanda, didn't want to be on the air, but his high-school coach and longtime friend, Buddy Baldwin, was great. It was like talking to an analyst. We were also able to get Mickey Bell, a former Carolina player who was a close friend of Roy, and that gave us another important perspective.

March 4, 2006 | Carolina 83, Duke 76

"Here's Frasor against Dockery. Trying to drive, backing up outside, shot clock at two, shot . . . good! A three by Hansbrough!"

I couldn't believe it when Tyler started to take the shot, and I believed it even less when it went in. What do they say—like the cherry on top of the sundae? That's exactly what that was. When it went in, Eric Montross started laughing on the air. I thought that was fitting because what better way to go over to Durham and kick

Duke's butt on senior night than to have the talented freshman throw in a three-pointer down the stretch? That was all we needed to make it the perfect evening.

It reminded me of when Carolina played in Durham in 1988 and Jeff Lebo was on crutches. The Blue Devil mascot tried to give him some roses or something—he wouldn't take them, which made me like him more—and the students started booing him because of it. Then Carolina proceeded to kick Duke's rear end all over Cameron Indoor Stadium. That was a great feeling because everyone knew the Tar Heels were already short-handed, and they still won the game.

January 6, 2008 | Carolina 90, Clemson 88 (OT)

"Ginyard will inbound for the Tar Heels along the right sideline. Holds it high, gets it in to Lawson. Here goes Lawson on the drive, gets it over to Ellington. Ellington with the jumper . . . good! Carolina wins!"

Wayne had a heck of a game that night. He had a big basket every time Carolina needed it. He let that shot go no more than 15 feet from in front of our broadcast position, and it was almost like we were looking straight down the line at it. There were times during my career that we had the best angle. That was the case that night—as soon as he let it go, we could tell it was perfect.

We didn't always have great views. Virginia seemed to be the place where we had the worst angles. The people there hated Carolina so much that they put a piece of tape down on the media table and would tell us not to cross over the tape. Ademola Okulaja made a game-winning three-pointer in Charlottesville in 1999, and I never saw him take the shot. I just saw the ball in the air. I sure saw the celebration, though.

April 6, 2009 | Carolina 89, Michigan State 72

*"How 'bout them Tar Heels! They are the national
champions!"*

When Coach Smith won his first national championship, I remember feeling a sense of relief. When he won his second one, boy,
that's when the good times rolled. That's how it was in 2009 with
Roy Williams. Because the game was not close down the stretch, we
were able to watch the reactions of players and coaches as they realized what was happening. To be honest, I was in a state of shock. I
didn't expect the game to be as convincing as it was, not against a
Tom Izzo–coached team.

I'll never forget watching the reaction of Tyler Hansbrough at
the end of the game, when he came running out on the court with
that giant smile on his face. That was a great window into how much
winning a title meant to that team.

Chapter 15

NCAA Issues

Coming off the basketball team's struggles during the 2009–10 season, the summer of 2010 was one of the most unsettled I can remember in Chapel Hill. It's one thing to suffer some losses on the basketball court and have to play in the NIT. It's quite another to have the NCAA on campus.

When Butch Davis was hired in the fall of 2006, I thought it was a perfect fit. Because of the reputation he had built at Miami, it was the most high-profile football hire Carolina had made since Jim Tatum. No one was concerned about Davis's struggles with the Cleveland Browns in the NFL. What excited Carolina fans was the fact that not only had he built an incredible storehouse of talent at Miami, but—ironically— he had also done it while cleaning up some NCAA issues that had long plagued the program in Coral Gables.

When he was hired, I didn't know him at all. That was fairly unusual during my Carolina career. Usually, if I didn't know a new coach personally, I at least knew someone who did. Anytime there was a new hire during my career, my immediate goal was simple: I had to gain his trust. The head football coach was someone I knew I would be around almost every day during the fall. He had to know that I wasn't going to do something to embarrass him and that I had a good feel for what he did and didn't want to talk about.

I think I gained Coach Davis's trust faster than I gained his friendship. By that, I mean he was comfortable that I was capable of doing the job up to his expectations. Many times, that type of trust evolves into a close friendship. I believe we were friends, but I wouldn't say we were close. I'm not sure he had many close friends in Chapel Hill. Butch told me early in his Carolina career, "Woody, I'm going to lean on you to help me understand the history and tradition of Carolina football." That was the last time we ever spoke about that subject. In general, Butch was not interested in tradition that predated any Tar Heel players currently in the NFL, unless it was Lawrence Taylor. He made it clear he considered the history of the Charlie Justice era, for example, to be substantially less important than the more recent years.

In the interim between his NFL experience and being hired at Carolina, Davis had done some work on television with the NFL Network. That gave him a unique viewpoint on how we should conduct interviews, radio shows, and television shows. John Bunting had been good on the air, but it had nothing to do with formal media training—it was his personality. Butch had training.

Early in his tenure, we were taping the television show and someone made a mistake. The producer said, "Just pick it up right there."

Before I could even lead him back into the segment, Butch said, "Three, two, one," and started right where he had left off.

He was the only football coach I ever worked with who had that kind of media savvy. From that standpoint, he was a natural. I saw it even after he left Carolina. A few months after he was fired, he produced a YouTube video addressing some of the questions about the NCAA investigation. I don't know many head coaches who would take the initiative—or have the interest—to do that. He came across on camera very well.

He ran the program much like a corporate executive. With past coaches, I had always handled setting up any interviews directly with the head coach. Under Butch, I went through Kevin Best, the football sports information director, just like the rest of the media. Butch never came out and said this, but I believe he put a higher value on spots with national media like ESPN than he did spots with the school radio network. That was his prerogative, and I can understand why from his perspective he might have felt that way. But it did not make my job any easier.

Head football and basketball coaches have contracts that require certain media obligations with the school's network. They get paid big money for those interviews. They also have little desire to devote the time we ask of them. It can create a difficult situation. As far back as Dick Crum, it could be a challenge. He originally did his radio show with John Kilgo because Kilgo had beaten Jim Heavner to the rights. Naturally, that prompted Heavner to start his own radio show, which became ACC Hotline. Calling George Welsh, the head coach at Virginia, to get an interview when I was the Carolina broadcaster was not easy. We eventually decided to send coaches $100 apiece for doing the show. The only one who refused us was Danny Ford at Clemson, who told us we had to pay him $200. We declined. By the end of my career, most coaches wouldn't have walked across the street for $100. The money in coaching has changed dramatically in the last five years.

Because I did not have a prior relationship with Butch, I tried to be careful about representing Carolina football the way I thought he would want. I wanted the time we spent together to be productive. As the relationship progressed, I got a feel for what he liked talking about and what he didn't like talking about, and that helped shape the broadcasts and our interactions more effectively.

It's rare that coaches get angry about something that is said on a broadcast during the game, because they rarely hear those comments (although Carolina did have one coach who made it a habit to either go back and listen to the broadcasts or have someone else listen to them for him). The games Butch Davis coached for the Tar Heels were almost always close, so there was never any real cause to say something objectionable during a blowout. That's when you can get in trouble as a school-affiliated broadcaster. I felt I had an obligation to the University of North Carolina. I was on the school-sponsored network, and the vast majority of listeners were Tar Heel fans. But if the score was 54–20, there weren't a whole lot of ways to paint that picture in a pretty way. Coaches don't always understand that. Sometimes, they think saying the score is negative. That's where coaches and media personnel can disagree. To someone in the media, the score is just a fact of the game. But coaches can see it as an indictment of their teams.

In the spring of 2010, however, no one had any cause to say anything negative about Carolina football. The program was coming off successive 8–5 seasons, and I thought the Tar Heels were ready to make the big jump to national prominence. The losses in 2009 had been close, including a 30–27 loss against Florida State, a 28–27 defeat to N.C. State in Raleigh, and a 19–17 loss to Pittsburgh in the Meineke Car Care Bowl. It looked like the talent to win some of the close games the Tar Heels had traditionally lost was finally on hand. The 2010 season opener was scheduled to be against national powerhouse LSU in Atlanta on national television. It seemed like the perfect stage to make that dramatic leap into the awareness of college football fans.

Then the NCAA investigation news broke. I had spent my entire life as a Carolina fan, and that was one of the first times I can ever remember the athletic department being in an embarrassing situation. Sometimes, it felt like a nightmare. It was incredibly unfortunate that the whole firestorm could be started by three selfish players who valued themselves more than they valued the University of North Carolina. In some ways, I wasn't surprised by the involvement of Marvin Austin and Greg Little. Watching their careers, it was clear they had some individualistic tendencies. Robert Quinn was the one who surprised me. He had been through so much just to get to Carolina, overcoming a brain tumor and coming back to play major-college football. He was soft-spoken and didn't seem like the type who would get mixed up with something he knew was wrong.

My question was simple: how could those three do that to their teammates, the program, and the school? I'm sure he won't remember it this way, but I consider that time period as Dick Baddour's shining moment as the athletic director at Carolina. There was no good way to handle that mess. But he did it with the character any Tar Heel fan would expect.

I was also disappointed by the reactions of some fans toward the UNC chancellor, Holden Thorp. Some of the comments I heard directed toward him from the fan base were embarrassing. Holden Thorp was a Tar Heel before many of the people involved in the NCAA investigation had ever heard of Chapel Hill. Holden Thorp will be a Tar Heel long after many of them are forgotten. Anyone who believes that Chancellor Thorp would do something to wrongfully harm the football program has a poor understanding of how much he cares about the university.

I remember flying back with him from the 2009 basketball national championship in Detroit. I described the scene he was about to witness in Chapel Hill and the way the fans would react to the team when it returned to the Smith Center. He was as excited as any fan—because he is a fan. But he's also a fan who has to do what is right with the entire university in mind. Most of us make decisions based on what is important to us. For some fans, that importance stops with sports. For Holden Thorp, it encompasses the entire school.

I believe the NCAA troubles will change the way Carolina relates to superstar athletes. Naturally, the initial reaction is to say that everyone should be treated the same way. That's not reality. The reality is that the best players are going to be more influenced by outsiders than are the less-famous players. Going forward, I think you'll see, both at Carolina and elsewhere, a higher level of scrutiny from athletic departments on the best players. It makes sense to try and give those individuals a different kind of awareness of things that can happen to them that have negative consequences both for them and for the program.

My concern was that, at the initial press conference, everyone at the podium vowed to clean up the problems. Then we all had to sit there and watch even more bad news continue to hit the papers. Once the initial investigation began, it seemed obvious that more problems would be found, and that those problems would be magnified because of the scrutiny. I'm not saying that it was right to have academic problems or to have an unusual number of parking tickets. But we are talking about a cross-section of 120 college students. If you pull any cross-section of 120 students out of any college in America, and you scrutinize every single thing that they've done during their time in college, you're probably going to find at least a few issues.

That doesn't excuse, however, the actions of someone like John Blake, the defensive line coach. Butch Davis said he was sorry he trusted John Blake. I was sorry, too. For years, many people worked very hard to make sure the University of North Carolina had a clean reputation as a school that did things the right way. The selfish actions of a few people cast a shadow on that reputation and caused months and years of distress for those who love the university.

I thought there were two possibilities: the coaching staff didn't have any idea that stuff was going on, or the coaching staff knew it was going on and chose to ignore it. It doesn't seem especially complicated to clean up something like parking tickets. Everett Withers made a simple rule, and everyone was aware of it: if a player received three parking tickets, his keys were taken away. That was a proactive policy with clear-cut consequences.

I don't remember ever specifically discussing the investigation with Coach Davis. In the entire 2010 season of television shows, we may have made two references to the situation. It was understood that wasn't a topic on which he wanted to spend a lot of time.

On our first radio broadcast of the season, in the pregame show for the LSU game, we talked about the NCAA investigation. It was by far the dominant issue involving Carolina football; we had to discuss it. I made a simple statement: "During this season, we're going to talk about the guys that are on the field. We're not going to talk about the guys that aren't on the field." That was the policy we tried to follow for the rest of the 2010 season. I think it was the right thing to do. The listeners didn't want to hear me repeatedly say, "Well, if it wasn't for those three selfish players, this season would be different." That would have insulted the listeners. They knew the circumstances.

Even without the missing players, Carolina was a good team. What I'll always wonder is how the three close games the Tar Heels lost might have been different. The first two losses of the season, to LSU and Georgia Tech, were by six points each. How might those games have gone with a full roster? Unfortunately, we'll never know, and that's a shame for the players and coaches who behaved and abided by the rules.

It was a challenge to do my job the same way I had done it for the previous 39 years. I was always a firm believer in preparation. Well, how could I prepare for a game when the players available changed on an almost daily basis? One of the fundamental parts of my game preparation was my spotter's board, which listed the two-deep depth charts for both teams. The board was a quick tool to find facts about certain players and also to help the spotter identify the player who made a play. It would have been almost impossible to do a new board every time I received new eligibility news about specific players. When there was a question about whether a certain player would be eligible, I left him on my spotter's board. If and when he was ruled ineligible, I put an X over his name.

By the time the 2010 season was finished, I had a lot of *X*s in prominent places on my board.

Memorable Moments

October 29, 2009 | Carolina 20, Virginia Tech 17

"Casey Barth with a 22-yard field goal off the right hash. Mark House on the snap, Trase Jones puts it down. Kick is up, it's good! Carolina has won the game, upsetting the nation's 14th-ranked team, stopping Virginia Tech's win streak at 12 here in Lane Stadium."

Those details about the win streak and the rankings were on my game card. I specifically remember putting that kind of stuff in for Virginia Tech. That particular night, I think I made a reference later on to Casey now being even with Connor. Now, both Barth brothers had won a big game with a field goal.

That's where preparation pays off. Those things I looked up, that I wasn't sure if I would ever use, ended up being important on the biggest play of the game.

Chapter 16

Retirement

I never considered retirement after the 2009 basketball championship.
That might seem strange, given that I retired two years later. But at the
time, Carolina was coming off titles in 2005 and 2009, and I honestly
thought I would see more of those championships in the years to come.

By the end of the next basketball season, in the spring of 2010, I gave
my first real consideration to retirement. I was not happy with my presentation of the games. I got some names incorrect, and it was really starting to bother me. It was especially noticeable to me in the nonconference
games, when I didn't have the same level of familiarity with the players. I
tried to improve my concentration, but that didn't help.

Over the summer of 2010, I made a conscious effort to change the
way I prepared for the nonconference games in November and December.
I thought perhaps some of the problem the previous season had been fa-
tigue, so I tried to pay more attention to getting rest in addition to being
prepared for every game. In my opinion, I showed some improvement
early in that season, but toward the latter part of the preconference schedule the problems began to surface again. Jones Angell and Eric Montross
were considerate. During timeouts, when we were in a commercial break,

they would sometimes correct me or point out a different pronunciation. I tried to accept their help and not let on how much it was bothering me that I was making mistakes. Every time they had to correct me, I was thinking, I can't believe I've done it again! The problem kept raising its ugly head.

Jean and I talked about it. I had recognized some problems the previous season and tried to take steps to correct those problems. It became apparent that even those steps were not working. I remembered something that Cawood Ledford, who did play-by-play for Kentucky for 39 years, had once told me: "When it's time, you'll know." That was when I realized that my body was telling me it was time. I didn't want to have to be carried kicking and screaming out of the broadcast booth.

I wasn't the only one who was pondering retirement. A few months later, I got an email from Dick Baddour after he announced his upcoming retirement. "I had really hoped to go out the way you did," he told me. I believe everyone likes to think of their retirement that way. We all want to imagine that we'll decide when it's time, not have someone else decide for us.

By the late fall of 2010, I had discussed it only with Jean. We went to Atlanta for Christmas, and the boys were there. It worked out that we had to go out on an errand. When we got in the car, I told them, "Let's drive around a little bit because I have something to ask you." I explained that I was considering retirement and wanted to get their opinions.

Wes's reply was, "Dad, I think your timing is great because you're going out on your terms."

That's the way I looked at it, too. It wasn't a decision I wanted someone else to make for me if they felt my performance was substandard.

Several years ago, Gary Sobba, the general manager at Tar Heel Sports Marketing, told me, "I hope the day never comes that you retire. But if it does, I hope you'll give us sufficient notice so that we can celebrate it the right way."

I had no interest in that. I didn't want it to be a big deal and distract from anything pertaining to the football and basketball seasons. I didn't want to go around to various ACC arenas and have people act like they

Woody and Jean
PERSONAL COLLECTION

Woody with his grandchildren, Will and Emily, in a photo that still hangs at Sutton's Drug Store on Franklin Street
PERSONAL COLLECTION

liked me and give me a rocking chair or some kind of retirement gift. That's why, even though I knew at Christmas that I was in my final season, I didn't tell a single person other than my family. Roy was in the middle of his season. Butch was preparing for a bowl game and then had a busy recruiting period. Dick Baddour was trying to run an athletic department. I didn't feel it was appropriate for me to add one more item to their lists of things to worry about, so I kept it to myself.

Since it was essentially a secret, it seems natural that I might have had second thoughts. Since no one really knew about it, it would have been easy to decide at a later time that maybe I wasn't ready for retirement just yet after all, and no one other than my family would have known any better. For some reason, though, that never crossed my mind. I felt I had made the decision. It wasn't something I wanted to second-guess. I trusted myself, I trusted Jean, and I trusted Wes and Taylor. We'd decided together. I wanted to stick to the decision we had made after careful consideration, rather than being swept up in an emotional moment.

After we talked, the only remaining football game was the Music City Bowl against Tennessee. That was a great one to do as my final game because it was so tight that there was absolutely no time to be sentimental about it being the last time. Seemingly every play in that game was important. The crazy ending, when T. J. Yates spiked the ball to give Carolina a chance to kick the game-tying field goal, was unlike anything I had seen before. Even after 40 years, you can never think you've seen everything, because in sports something new is always right around the corner.

Our postgame routine was always for me to go down to the locker room to interview the head coach as soon as the game was over. And that's what I did after Carolina won the game 30–27. That was a happy team and a happy coach, so I had no time to think, I won't be doing this again.

I also knew it wasn't really the end because the conference basketball season was approaching. The end of basketball did feel different. That's when I really got the sense that it was over. For that team to survive all the personnel losses was impressive. The Tar Heels made it to the regional final against Kentucky, and I was really hoping they'd get to go to another Final Four. But after broadcasting for 40 years, I'm well aware that getting to a Final Four is difficult. Sometimes, good teams don't make it. That's what happened to Carolina in 2011.

That's when it hit me that it was over. Even then, in March, I still hadn't told Dick Baddour or anyone other than my family. So I had the disappointment of losing the game and the team missing out on the Final Four, but I also knew it was the last game I would do. I tried not to let that come through on the air. I didn't want people around the water cooler the next day to say, "Hey, I heard Woody say this on the radio last night. What do you think he was trying to say?" I didn't want what I was doing to be a distraction from what the team had accomplished.

To be honest, I'm a little surprised that I didn't let it slip to anyone. After the basketball season, one of the first people I told was John Montgomery, the executive director of the Rams Club. I wanted to get his advice. I didn't want to retire from play-by-play radio broadcasting and have everyone assume I never wanted to be associated with Carolina again. I enjoyed getting out and doing the Rams Club meetings and talking with the fans and the coaches. I wanted to know if John thought I would have an opportunity to continue doing that type of thing.

John has been in the college sports business for a long time. He gave me some good advice: if I was retiring, I also had to stop doing free appearances. He explained that I needed a rate card, and that groups needed to understand that they would have to pay me in order for me to give a speech. That was difficult for me. I didn't want anyone to think I was trying to take advantage of them. But at the same time, I didn't want anyone to take advantage of me either. Wes's agent helped formulate a rate card. Most groups have been understanding because I make it clear to them that since I'm not employed by Tar Heel Sports Properties anymore, this is how I'm making a living.

After speaking with John, I told Dick Baddour, Gary Sobba, Roy Williams, and Butch Davis. I also telephoned the chancellor and made Doug Dibbert from the General Alumni Association aware. As a supplement to my contract with Learfield—the corporation that operates Tar Heel Sports Properties—Dick had been gracious enough to arrange an athletic department subsidy. We discussed whether that could continue;

he said there wasn't room in the budget to make it happen. I still want to talk to Bubba Cunningham, the new athletic director, about some ways I believe I can help the athletic department. I believe there is interest in the smaller communities that don't get the Tar Heel Tour in having a Carolina contingent come see them. I'd love to go with Bubba on the road and stop in five or six midsize towns and talk about the Tar Heels. I've been surprised that Learfield has expressed little interest in structuring something for me to work on part-time.

Before Jones Angell was hired, Gary Sobba asked me, "Depending on who we hire, would you be willing to work with them to ease their transition?" I told him of course I would, but I never heard from him again. I'm glad that I was part of the pregame shows during the 2011–12 season and was able to do a feature for each show. But I also feel like maybe I didn't make it clear to everyone that I was just retiring from play-by-play on the radio network. I wasn't retiring from UNC.

Initially, we didn't set a date for the announcement. Eventually, we decided on April 20. As the date approached, Carolina was waiting on some important news from Harrison Barnes about whether he was turning pro. I was ready to move the date for my announcement if Harrison hadn't decided. Luckily, Harrison announced earlier in the week that he was returning to school, and we held the press conference as scheduled.

I was so grateful that Coach Williams made a special effort to come back from his recruiting trip. He had been in Texas the previous day and was headed to Florida, but he arranged to be in Chapel Hill for the announcement. That was special to me. It shows what kind of person he is.

I was a little uncomfortable that we held a press conference rather than simply putting out a statement. That had been my original plan. But Dick Baddour and Steve Kirschner, the associate A.D. for athletic communications, thought it would be important to the fans to have a press conference. I was not anticipating the large crowd that attended—not just media members, but coaches and staff members from the athletic department and many friends. It showed what a great place Carolina really is, and that the family you hear about truly does exist. People were complimentary about my career and said and wrote some nice things.

Wes Durham, Jim Nantz of CBS Sports, and Woody
PERSONAL COLLECTION

I knew as soon as the initial surprise wore off—and we did a good job keeping the secret, if I do say so myself—speculation would begin about the next play-by-play broadcaster for the Tar Heels. Because of Wes's position with Georgia Tech and the fact that people at Carolina were familiar with his work, I felt his name would probably be mentioned right away.

When we talked about my retirement in December, Wes and I had not discussed the possibility of him doing the Carolina games. It would be untrue to say I had never considered that he might take over for me. Any father would think that about his son. When I retired, Wes was in an unusual situation with Georgia Tech because the school was trying to transition him from full-time employment to a contract basis. He and Tony Barnhart were in the second year of establishing their new radio show. And in 2010, Wes had experienced his first conflict with Georgia Tech football and Falcons football. The Yellow Jackets played in the Independence Bowl in Shreveport on the same day the Falcons had an important Monday-night game. A variety of possibilities were discussed. Someone suggested the Falcons could send a jet to Shreveport to pick up Wes and get him back to Atlanta in time to broadcast the second half of the Falcons game. It turned into an issue that was even discussed in the Atlanta paper.

Wes called and asked for my advice. I told him I didn't think it could be settled without involving Arthur Blank, the Atlanta owner, and Dan Radakovich, the Georgia Tech athletic director. Finally, the Atlanta general manager, Rich McKay, told Wes that his contract called for him to do Georgia Tech games in case of a conflict, and that he should honor his contract. But McKay also said he planned to correct that provision in future contracts. So Wes was dealing with multiple different contracts in Atlanta. And in the periods of his worst frustration with that situation, I think he was open to coming to Chapel Hill.

I don't know if that ever could have happened. It would have been difficult for Wes to make the same amount of money at Carolina that he was making with his multiple contracts in Atlanta. It never got to that point. As the search was getting under way, Wes had dinner with a Learfield senior vice president, Steve Gowan. There was no job offer. There was no discussion of whether Wes was interested. I'm not sure it was handled the right way by Learfield, but that's how the company chose to do it. That doesn't mean it ever could have worked out with Wes. He would have wanted to be a full-time employee of the university rather than Learfield, and that might have been difficult to arrange. In the end, there were just too many hurdles on both sides to make it happen.

At that point, I felt Jones Angell was the logical choice. The search came down to Jones and three outside candidates. Gary Sobba asked me to listen to some of the clips they had submitted as part of their applications. The other three had some good qualities, but I didn't feel they offered anything outstanding. Apparently, it's Learfield policy that when it hires someone, it wants to hear a long stretch of one game, rather than a series of highlights from multiple games. Personally, I would rather hear the highlights. I want to hear a broadcaster in many different situations, from big, game-winning plays to disappointing, heartbreaking losses. But that's not how Learfield handles the hiring process.

I also met with Dick Baddour during the search. It was pretty obvious that the decision would be between Jones and one outside candidate. But the outside candidate had absolutely no familiarity with Carolina at all. I didn't believe that would work. I didn't think the fan base would allow an outsider to make mistakes and still be willing to stick with him. I didn't feel Jones would have a difficult time adjusting to the job at all. But if he did, I thought the fact that he was already known as a Tar Heel by the fans would give him a little cushion. I left that meeting feeling that even if Learfield was looking at outside candidates, Dick was sold on Jones and understood my point about the value of having some Carolina history in the job. It's ultimately a job representing UNC. That's why I felt Dick's endorsement was important, and that Jones would ultimately be the pick.

I was on vacation when Jones was officially announced as the new play-by-play man. On the second day after Jean and I came back, I met with him. He asked to see my drive chart and score chart from football. I was happy to help him in any way I could. I also wanted to find out a little more about his plans for handling the broadcasts. For example, in football, charting the game is beneficial in helping you tell the story, but

Woody receiving UNC's Distinguished Service Medal. Charles Kuralt is second from the right.

At a halftime ceremony during the 2011–12 basketball season, Woody was honored as the football radio booth was named after him. From left to right are Governor Beverly Purdue, Jean Durham, Woody, former UNC athletic director Dick Baddour, current UNC athletic director Bubba Cunningham, and UNC chancellor Holden Thorp.
PHOTO BY JEFFREY A. CAMARATI

Ed Crutchfield, former CEO of First Union Bank, introducing Woody at his induction into the Stanly County Hall of Fame
PERSONAL COLLECTION

it's also a little like patting your head and rubbing your stomach at the same time. I also wanted to make sure he felt a certain comfort level in the booth. When we met, I told him, "There is no one in that booth who doesn't know you and you don't know them. You are not a stranger to anybody. It's ready-made for you to step in and do the broadcast the way you want to do it."

Jones was fortunate that he had a good background in the business and also knew a variety of broadcasters to go to for advice. I know Wes gave him some pointers, and I'm sure he has talked to Mick Mixon regularly.

What Carolina fans will see from Jones is that he will do nothing but get better. That's because he will be more comfortable in the job. His second year will be better than his first year because he'll have a better idea of what works and what doesn't work.

I didn't listen to any of the football broadcasts straight through during his first year, but I heard pieces of some of them. Ideally, over the summer, I would like to tell Jones to bring me copies of the best game he thought he did in his first season in both sports. We'll listen to them, and if the broadcasts couldn't be improved, I'll tell him that. But if there's anything I could possibly help him with, we'll talk about it and figure out if he wants to do anything differently in his second year. I think that's a way I can help him.

I still get questions from young broadcasters who want to know how they should get started in the business. I tell them the same thing I told Wes: start with a résumé of practical experience. If you want to be an announcer, get a job at any local television or radio station you can find. Work with the promotions department and the sales department because you'll be dealing with them every day if you're an announcer.

Beyond the practical experience, the key is to work. Write for the school newspaper. If you don't play on the team, do the PA for high-school basketball and football games. Get as heavy a dose of real-world experience as you can possibly find. Be persistent in trying to get your foot in the door somewhere. Eventually, that will turn into an opportunity. Be willing to take opportunities when they are presented to you.

Woody and Jean with their grandchildren, Will and Emily

My game day is very different now. I don't regret my retirement. That doesn't mean that I don't miss the job—a lot. But retirement has given me the opportunity to see football Saturdays and basketball game days in a different way. I always said that when I retired, I wanted to be a part of the tailgating scene around Chapel Hill. It didn't take me long to learn that it is a special part of a Saturday in town. Can you imagine that I went to every football game for 40 years and never took part in a pregame tailgate?

In 2011, I was fortunate to be part of a group that tailgates near the Bell Tower. I never realized how many people walk up Stadium Drive to get to the game, and I was gratified that so many of them stopped to say hello to me. That was a special part of the opening football game in 2011, which was the first time I hadn't been behind the microphone in 40 years.

It wasn't until I walked into the stadium that I considered how different it was going to be. The Rams Club's Ken Mack was nice enough to get Jean and me seats in the Blue Zone, which is a magnificent facility. It was the first day for the Blue Zone, and I enjoyed looking around. Once the game started, though, and once it was obvious Carolina had a good team, I started missing broadcasting.

I miss the game days, but I don't miss the preparation. That's true for both football and basketball. At the first home basketball game of the 2011–12 season, I was struck by the fact that it was the first time anyone other than me had ever called a Carolina game in the Smith Center.

It was time for someone else to fill that role, though. I still want to be a part of Carolina. It doesn't have to be in the athletic department. It could be any part of the university. A capable group is running the university and the athletic department right now. People who are around him on a regular basis rave about Bubba Cunningham. Larry Fedora has energized the football program.

I believe those two have the most important challenge facing Carolina athletics right now. We have to bring football back. Bubba and Larry have

Opposite page: *Woody and Jean*
PERSONAL COLLECTION

to unify the fan base because right now there is a substantial split. The unhappiness over the end of the Butch Davis era was bigger than I ever imagined. I never thought certain people would stop giving money to the academic side of the university because of a football decision. That's not supposed to be who we are. If you're with us, you're supposed to understand that what's done is done with the idea of the best interests of the entire institution.

The rest of the sports, in my opinion, are on a solid foundation. But the reality of college sports today is that you need a healthy football program to sustain those other sports. Carolina is in a unique position because it has the luxury of a revenue-producing basketball program. Many schools don't have that. But everyone in Chapel Hill realizes the university must have high-quality football to go with the basketball.

I have loved my association with the university. It was around 1977, when I moved to Cary, that someone first said to me, "Woody, when I hear your voice, I think of Carolina." I loved it when people said that. Sometimes, I got the feeling that some in the athletic department—not the coaches, but other people—might be offended by that idea. I never understood that. I didn't ask for that kind of attention. On one occasion, a writer who had worked closely with the university before being fired for some email indiscretions implied that I thought I was bigger than the games. How could that be possible? My job was to describe the games. You can't have an announcer without games.

I took an immense amount of pride in my association with Carolina. I believe the University of North Carolina is the greatest institution in the world. Who wouldn't be proud to be associated with it? In second grade, when I was running around in a Charlie Justice uniform pretending to be Choo Choo, if I had been told that one day people would approach me and ask for my autograph, I never would have believed it. Early in the 2011–12 basketball season, Tar Heel Sports Properties distributed CDs with some of my famous calls. At the game when they were distributed, several fans approached me and asked me to sign them. A couple of them said, "You'll always be Carolina to me." In a way, I guess that's what I was always working for. But at the same time, I wasn't working for it, if that makes any sense.

It was an outcome of 40 years of trying to do the best job I could for Carolina athletics, and being fortunate enough to broadcast the games of some fantastic coaches and players. Fans wouldn't have any idea who Woody Durham is if it wasn't for the opportunity I had to describe some of the most memorable moments of their lives. No matter where they were, they felt like they were right there with me watching the game—just a couple of Carolina fans together, hoping for a Tar Heel victory. I was lucky to be courtside or in the press box for those games, and I feel privileged to have shared those experiences with every listener.

Memorable Moments

December 30, 2010 | Carolina 30, Tennessee 27

"Straight away, the ball equidistant between the two sidelines. Snap, spot, kick, good! Carolina wins! The Tar Heels win the Music City Bowl 30–27 in a game that will be discussed for a long, long time. And nobody is celebrating more than quarterback T. J. Yates."

That game was the capper on T. J. Yates's career. It was the perfect way for him to go out. I was fortunate to look at the clock exactly when he spiked the ball, and I saw there was one second left. And to have it be T. J. who made the play made it even more special.

I felt like I had a good relationship with T. J. Anyone who knew the story of what he had been through at Carolina had to appreciate it when he walked off the field in Nashville as the hero.

Acknowledgments

Since I stepped away from the broadcast of Carolina football and basketball in April of 2011 after 40 years and more than 1,800 games, the obvious question has been, "How are you enjoying retirement?"

"So far, so good," has been my standard reply.

However, a lot of fans also want to know, "Do you miss it?"

Of course I do. You can't do something you like doing, despite the preparation that was required, and not miss it. The excitement of game days, especially for big games, was special. Yet it was impossible to enjoy the game days if I wasn't prepared to my satisfaction.

I heard a frequent question during the time I was calling the play-by-play: "When are you going to write a book?" This was often asked after I spoke at various functions and told stories about games, coaches, and players. I wanted to wait until I retired, so the time is now.

Never having written a book, I needed help, so I asked Adam Lucas to provide it. He agreed. He still remembers me helping him with a high-school paper, although I didn't really offer much help. Adam has matured as an excellent writer about the Tar Heels and become a master organizer. I marvel at his ability within a short time after a game to post a GoHeels.com column that is both informative and entertaining to read.

Adam had written five previous books about Carolina and came to our first meeting with a detailed outline of the proposed chapters for my book. We then met 16 times over the next 17 weeks. Each time, he would submit an advance list of questions dealing with a particular chapter, and then he would interview me for at least an hour, if not longer, and put the chapters together. He's at the top of my thank-you list.

John F. Blair, Publisher, of Winston-Salem also gets my thanks. This is one of the few true sports books Blair has published, and I hope it meets the company's expectations.

Many, many others deserve my gratitude, including those I grew up with and around Albemarle and during my four years at Carolina. Most notable are Jake Presson of radio station WZKY, who gave me the opportunity to start my broadcast career a week before my 16th birthday, and football coach Toby Webb, who molded championship teams including the 1957 Bulldogs.

I knew I wasn't good enough or big enough to play at the next level, so I decided on a career in sports broadcasting. I was able to get plenty of experience in Chapel Hill with both WUNC-TV and radio station WCHL.

After I graduated in 1963, a short stay with WBTW-TV in Florence, South Carolina, set me up to become sports director at WFMY-TV in Greensboro. C. D. Chesley, the producer of ACC basketball, recommended me for the position and later gave me the opportunity to be part of the weekly ACC television package. General managers Gaines Kelley and Bill Gietz also allowed me to do some regional radio broadcasts of Wake Forest and Guilford football in the fall before getting to ACC basketball in the winter.

The work of photographer Grady Allred and sportscaster Johnny Phelps allowed us to have the area's top-rated sportscasts. That dominance continued when I started following the Tar Heels in 1971. I worked at Channel 2 for six more years before leaving the Triad for the Triangle.

Recently, Jack Hilliard, my producer-director at WFMY-TV and a Carolina classmate, has initiated his personal support of my career. His efforts earned me the Chris Schenkel Award from the National Football

Foundation. Now, he has nominated me for the Curt Gowdy Award from the Naismith Basketball Hall of Fame. I greatly appreciate his efforts.

Durham Life Broadcasting was a solid radio operation. President Carl Venters, who worked at Channel 4 when I was in college, got the company into TV with the purchase of WRDU and gave me a chance to come help build up the UHF/NBC affiliate. A new tower allowed the station to make some progress, but the demands of the Tar Heel Sports Network for additional programming prompted my move to the parent Village Companies in 1981.

Dr. Homer Rice was the UNC athletic director when I followed Bill Currie in 1971 as the voice of the Tar Heels. I eventually worked with three more athletic bosses: Bill Cobey, John Swofford, and Dick Baddour. Five different sports information directors—Jack Williams, Rick Brewer, Steve Kirschner, Kevin Best, and Matt Bowers—were a big help.

Bob Quincy, a noted Charlotte sportswriter, was my first color announcer when the rights holder was the G. H. Johnston Agency in New York. Dick Frick was the general manager. There would be five more after the rights shifted to the Village Companies and then to Learfield Sports, based in Jefferson City, Missouri. They were Dianne Smith, Chris Bolton, Tim Noonan, Bill Whitley, and Gary Sobba.

Quincy was with the network for only a year before being hired by the *Charlotte Observer*. He was followed by a slew of analysts and color announcers including UNC legend Charlie "Choo Choo" Justice, several other former UNC standouts, and Lee Kinard, a Greensboro TV personality. Once Chapel Hill's Jim Heavner secured the rights in 1977, he worked the games before moving Bob Holliday into the booth. Then came Draggan Mihailovich, Henry Hinton, Freddie Kiger, and Mick Mixon. A Chapel Hill native, Mick spent 16 years with the network before joining the NFL's Carolina Panthers as the play-by-play announcer.

I thank more recent analysts such as Rick Steinbacher and Ken Mack in football and Phil Ford and Eric Montross in basketball. Stephen Gates and Lee Pace worked the sidelines. After just six years as the network host, Jones Angell has now moved into the play-by-play seat.

I benefited from the work of several outstanding spotters. Harold

Bowen, who started out in 1971 along with his twin brother, Carroll, was with me for 30 years. Whitey Smith filled in for a few years, then Eric Fiddleman joined the crew. When the crew was reduced from six to five along the front row of the Kenan booth, Jody Zeugner added spotting to his responsibilities as statistician. Then Greg Tilley filled in for Zeugner during the 2010 season.

Ben Alexander has been the network engineer for the past seven years. He follows a long list of contributors dating back to 1971—Rick Edwards, Jim and Patti Eddings, David Wright, Jerry Brown, David Modlin, Fred Pace, Paul Boone, David Horn, and John Rose.

In addition to the radio broadcasts, I handled the coaches' weekly TV shows. Grady Allred, Clyde Knight, Gary Otto, and Chris Schleter worked with me in the 1970s. Then came Bob Ellis, Ken Cleary, Jason Andrews, and Michael Crowe more recently.

During my 40 years, I worked with six different head football coaches and their staffs. Among them, Bill Dooley, Dick Crum, Mack Brown, Carl Torbush, John Bunting, and Butch Davis had nearly 900 lettermen—including 19 first-team All-Americans—in their programs. The head coaches' secretaries were mighty important for what I needed to get done with their bosses. My thanks to Lilly Turner, Betty King, Becky Medford, Maria Smith, Teresa Vanderford, and Pamela Higley.

I also worked with four different basketball coaches and their staffs. Dean Smith, Bill Guthridge, Matt Doherty, Roy Williams, and their 200 lettermen—including 33 All-Americans—made what I tried to do for them pretty easy. Again, the secretaries—Betsy Terrell, Linda Woods, Jennifer Holbrook, and Nadia Lynch—were a big help.

Together, the two programs won 72 percent of the 1,805 games I had the opportunity to broadcast. That made me sound pretty good on a lot of Saturday afternoons and cold winter nights.

Of course, I must thank those who have been closest to me.

For 49 years, my wife, Jean, has been a great partner as well as a wonderful mother and grandmother.

Our older son, Wes, has been a great success broadcasting Georgia Tech and the NFL's Atlanta Falcons.

Our daughter-in-law, Vicky, has been such an inspiration to Wes as well as an ultimate supporter of our grandchildren.

Our granddaughter, Emily, is thoughtful, talented, and a lover of animals.

Our grandson, Will, is humorous and caring and has such a positive attitude.

Our younger son, Taylor, has such loyalty and perseverance, which put him back at Elon as the school's broadcaster.

Our friends, old and new, as well as loyal and respectful Tar Heel fans have been the foundation of a truly happy life.

W. D.

As a sophomore in high school, I was assigned to do a biographical-type paper on someone I considered to be important to my life. I made an obvious choice: Woody Durham, who had been the radio voice of the Tar Heels for my entire life. He'd been the soundtrack of my formative years as a Carolina fan, and I chose him as my subject partly as an excuse to meet him. When I went to the Village Companies to interview Woody and his broadcast partner, Mick Mixon, I thought I'd reached the highest honor any Tar Heel fan could achieve.

Twenty years later, after working closely with Woody covering the Tar Heels over the course of the past 10 years, I'm well aware that helping with his book is recording Carolina history. This book is about his life, but for many of us it's also about an era of Tar Heel sports—one that we heard through him. The writer in me is grateful to Woody, Jean, Wes, and Taylor for the opportunity to help with this project. The fan in me is amazed I got to sit and listen to the incredible stories of the past 40 years of Carolina history.

John F. Blair, Publisher, was immediately excited about this project. A story about the quintessential Tar Heel should be told by only a North Carolina company, and Carolyn Sakowski and her staff were the perfect partners.

The staff at *Tar Heel Monthly*—Helen Buchanan, Grant Halverson, and Turner Walston—covered for me when Woody and I were trying to finish the book during basketball season. Lauren Brownlow tirelessly transcribed days' worth of interviews and provided input on the story's direction. Ben Alexander, Matt Bowers, Steve Kirschner, John Lyon, and Eric Montross were present for many of the best stories in this book and occasionally helped fill in some details. Jones Angell will have his own book to write in 40 years (Chapter Eleven: My Day with Berlingo). Until then, I'm happy he was able to provide advice on the best way to formulate this one.

My parents, Jim and Dubba Lucas, introduced me to the magic of Woody Durham and fueled my obsession with Carolina athletics, which I'm sure they only occasionally regret.

For many years, my ideal day involved a Carolina game at the Smith Center or a Saturday at Kenan Stadium. My wife, Stephanie, has introduced me to the idea—one that normal, balanced individuals apparently learned long ago—that an even more idyllic day can be spent on the beach or in the mountains or maybe even at home. Together, we've figured out something even more fulfilling than a national championship: watching Asher dive on the floor for a rebound or McKay perform in *The Nutcracker* . . . perhaps with Woody Durham describing the action.

A. L.

Appendix

Honored Tar Heel Players

I was privileged to call games played by hundreds of terrific Tar Heels who represented the University of North Carolina magnificently, in addition to winning a lot of games. During my career, I covered 16 of the 26 players who have received honored jerseys in Kenan Stadium and 31 of the 47 who have their jerseys in the rafters of the Smith Center.

No one would ever want to make a list of favorite teams or players. We're fortunate in Chapel Hill in having too many great players to list. But I do consider it a special privilege to have been able to watch these honored Tar Heels play.

Football

Harris Barton, 1983–86

Harris invited me to his draft-day party in 1987. It was unique to watch him get the phone call from a representative of the San Francisco 49ers before the team picked, then watch on television as the team publicly announced the selection. He was a terrific young man who I enjoyed getting to know.

After he had so much success with the 49ers, Harris decided he wanted to give something back to Carolina. He called Coach Smith for advice, but this was the pre-cell-phone era, and Coach Smith was out of his office. Within 10 minutes, Harris got a call back from Coach Smith, who was in an airport and had gotten the message. Harris asked for some guidance on where he should give the money. Coach Smith told him it might be beneficial to do something for a part of the university that helped people. So Harris gave a donation to the school of social work. A conference room in that school's new building is named for Harris Barton's father. I thought it was perceptive for a football player to be that caring about the university and the community as a whole.

Harris was a part of three Super Bowl champions. He told me that in Super Bowl XXII, before the 49ers went on their game-winning 92-yard drive, Joe Montana huddled the team around him before the first play. "Hey, H. B.," Montana said. "Isn't that John Mellencamp in the corner of the end zone?" Harris said he leaned out of the huddle, and sure enough, it was. "Good," Montana said. "Y'all keep them off me, and we'll win the game."

Brian Blados, 1980–83

He was part of the 1983 team that set a total offense record. That was an underrated group. He also had some success in the NFL.

Dré Bly, 1996–98

He was the only player to be first-team All-ACC for three years. He might have been the only defensive back I've ever seen who had such an incredible knack for where the ball was going to be. He had a game-changing interception against Virginia, his home-state team, in 1997. He was so alert and was an incredible athlete. After a long pro football career that included 43 interceptions, he's done a nice job trying to help people both in his hometown and in our area with a charity golf tournament.

Kelvin Bryant, 1979–82

He had the best combination of speed and power that I've ever seen in a Carolina back. He was quiet, but when the game started he got the job done. He's the only player Carolina ever touted on the cover of a media guide for the Heisman Trophy, which looked prophetic when he scored 15 touchdowns in the first three games of his final season. It makes no difference what else happens in the Carolina–East Carolina series. When people think of those games, they will always talk about Kelvin Bryant's six touchdowns in 1981.

To this day, you can often find him on the sidelines at Carolina games. He doesn't say much. He's friendly but doesn't make a big deal out of being Kelvin Bryant.

Greg Ellis, 1994-97

He was part of some of the best defenses Carolina ever had. During his final two seasons, the Tar Heels were 21–3. The team finished second nationally in yards allowed during his senior year. Both on and off the field, he was exactly what you wanted a Carolina football player to be. I was always impressed with the way he carried himself and the way he responded to success.

William Fuller, 1980-83

William Fuller was one of the best Carolina football players I've ever been around. An All-American two years in a row, he was quick as a cat. What made him so refreshing was that he was just as solid off the field. He played 15 years of professional football. I never doubted that he would be a success.

Dee Hardison, 1974-77

A terrific football player, he was picked in the second round of the NFL Draft. I thought he was a first-round talent. He was an All-American in 1977, when Carolina led the conference in scoring defense, giving up only 7.4 points per game. He played 11 years in the NFL before back problems forced him to retire.

Ethan Horton, 1981–84

Unusual circumstances saw him moved to tailback. He started at Carolina as a quarterback. Before the Tar Heels played at Maryland in 1981, the coaching staff asked him if he'd consider switching to tailback. He said, "Yes, if I can start." When he started and ran for 94 yards in a 17–10 win, it was obvious he was in the right position. He had a hard time getting started with his NFL career but ended up being an important player for the Oakland Raiders and Washington Redskins.

Ken Huff, 1972–74

He was an All-American guard in 1974 on an offense that totaled more than 4,700 yards. That was when Boom Boom Betterson and Mike Voight each got over 1,000 yards. He also won the Jacobs Blocking Trophy and went on to spend 11 years in the NFL. He's still very much around the Carolina football program. In my opinion, he should be in the College Football Hall of Fame.

Marcus Jones, 1992–95

Ken Browning was coaching the defensive line when Marcus played. They really liked each other. Ken once told me the secret to getting the best out of Marcus Jones was not screaming at him in practice. Ken tried to advise professional coaches when Marcus went to the NFL that he would go into a shell if they yelled at him.

Well, guess what Marcus ended up doing after football. The guy who didn't want anyone to yell at him became an Ultimate Fighter.

Amos Lawrence, 1977–80

Having him on the field at the same time with Kelvin Bryant might have been as good a backfield as it's possible to have. I thought that was the best combination I'd seen. He had 1,000 yards in each of his four seasons. Only six other players have done that in all of college football. I'm not sure he's been honored as much as he should have been at Carolina.

Julius Peppers, 1999–2001

He was—and is—a lot of fun to watch. What an athlete! You could sometimes see that athleticism even more on the basketball court, where he helped Carolina to the 2000 Final Four and the 2001 regular-season ACC championship. As a basketball player, he was a physical specimen who intimidated teams with his size and speed.

On the football field, I think there will always be a question about what his stats would have looked like if he gave 100 percent on every single play. Sometimes when players are so gifted, they know they can get by with a little less than full effort.

Ron Rusnak, 1970–72

Ron was the first All-American I was able to cover once I began calling the Carolina games. Bill Dooley's offense loved to run the ball, and Ron was an outstanding offensive guard. He won the Jacobs Blocking Trophy even though he wasn't all that big—only six-foot-two and 220 pounds. That's very different from the size you'd need today to play that position. One of his coaches once told me, "Ron may not be big, but he has the best technique of any offensive lineman I ever coached."

Brian Simmons, 1994–97

He was a smart football player, so it's no surprise he's in scouting for the NFL. I've been able to talk to him at some practices. He says scouting comes naturally because he has a good idea of what a player needs at the next level. If only he had scored on that interception return at Virginia in 1996, there's no telling how things might have changed for Carolina football.

Lawrence Taylor, 1977–80

Now, people think of him as a dominant player. But when he arrived at Carolina, the coaches couldn't figure out the right position for him. They tried him as a down lineman and a stand-up linebacker. It wasn't until Carolina won at N.C. State in 1979 that he really started getting some publicity. It was like someone flipped the light switch. He was terrific the rest of the season. And I'm not sure Carolina has ever had a player as dominating as he was in his senior year.

I still didn't realize the impact he was going to have on the NFL, though. One night, I was watching *SportsCenter*. The Giants were about to play the Cowboys. Tom Landry said, "Whenever you play the Giants, you have to change a lot of things because of Lawrence Taylor." I didn't know until then that the pros considered him that kind of player.

Of course, there are some off-the-field stories about him. In his book, he wrote about climbing up the side of Ehringhaus Dorm. He was hardly the only player who did that. Some of his problems have been really disappointing. It's sad to see a guy with that kind of talent who didn't do everything possible to be a great player.

Mike Voight, 1973–76

Everyone knew him as "the Space Cowboy." He might have been a little different, but he could really run the ball. He finished his career with 3,971 yards and would have been only the second back at Carolina to rush for 4,000 yards. He missed it because he was suspended for the Ohio State game in 1975 after he missed curfew one night that week. He later said he had a headache and went out to get some aspirin. When his parents came to the next home game, his mother brought a giant jar of aspirin and told him, "Now, you won't have to go out late anymore." Mike passed away in May 2012.

Basketball

Vince Carter, 1995–98

He had significant physical talent, but he also owes a big debt of gratitude to Coach Smith for his career. He learned how to play basketball at North Carolina.

Even other coaches marveled at him. In 1998, when Bill Guthridge was the Carolina head coach, Carter had a good game in Atlanta against

Georgia Tech and Bobby Cremins. Bobby, always a great quote, said, "You know who has the best deal going right now? Coach Smith. He's over at his house watching the game on TV, and I'm here at the game and I'm getting my butt kicked by guys like Vince Carter, who is trying to dunk on us all the time."

Bill Chamberlain, 1969-72

In the very first basketball game I ever did for Carolina, against Rice at Carmichael, Bill was suspended for breaking a team rule. But in 1971, when Dennis Wuycik went down against UMass, Bill Chamberlain basically picked Carolina up and carried it to the NIT championship. I'm glad that team was honored during the 2010–11 season. Fans today may not understand what an achievement it was to win the NIT in 1971. If nothing else, though, I know they appreciate that Carolina had to beat Duke to do it. In fact, the Tar Heels beat the Blue Devils three times that season.

Brad Daugherty, 1982-86

He does ESPN commentary for NASCAR now. Someone once asked me if I knew he was such a big NASCAR fan. My response was, "Well, look at his jersey number." He wore 43, which was also Richard Petty's number.

Brad came to Carolina even younger than the typical college freshman. The coaches worked with him on not bringing the ball down to where little guards could swipe it. They wanted him to hold it above his head. Once he figured that out, he was terrific.

He spoke at a ceremony in Asheville honoring Roy Williams and told a great story. When Brad was in college, he received some punishment from the team for failing to attend a class. Coach Smith told him he had to run from Carmichael Auditorium to Finley Golf Course each morning. The punishment was slated to begin the first day of spring break, so he thought he was going to get out of it for that day. At 7 a.m., the doorbell rang at his house back in the mountains. Brad looked out the window and saw a blue Mustang sitting in the driveway. It was Roy Williams's car.

He opened the door, and Coach Williams said, "You ready?" Brad said he ran all over Asheville while Coach Williams followed him in that Mustang, reading the paper the entire way.

Walter Davis, 1973-77

Walter's first start was a game in Charlotte. He sent manager Greg Miles out before the game. Greg said, "Walter wanted me to ask you a favor. He's listed on the roster as being from Charlotte. He's really from Pineville, and that's what he'd like you to use as his hometown on the radio." That's what I did. I later got thank-you letters from the Pineville mayor, the Pineville Chamber of Commerce, and several other people from Pineville. That's the kind of person Walter is. He wanted the people who had gotten him to that point to get the credit for it.

Phil Ford once said about Walter, whose nickname was "Sweet D," "He is so smooth. Even when he dances, he's smooth."

Walter will always be remembered for the shot against Duke in 1974.

Wayne Ellington, 2006-09

I was so impressed with the way he played. Even on his off nights, and he didn't have many, he kept trying to make it happen. In Detroit in the championship game against Michigan State, he was about as good as it gets. The shot that will always stick out to me is the three-pointer he made on the left wing. That's when I knew the rout was on.

Raymond Felton, 2002-05

He was close to Matt Doherty because of the recruiting process. A lot of players would have gone south with the coaching change, but he didn't let that happen. To become the player he was under Roy Williams said a lot about him. The three-pointer he made against Illinois in the national championship game in 2005 was a big-time shot.

Phil Ford, 1974-78

Carolina fans have a love affair with Phil Ford. Phil's mother told a funny story about Coach Smith visiting their home during the recruiting process. When he left, Phil's mother said, "Wasn't that nice of Carolina to send a dean to see little Phil?" She never saw him play, by the way—never in high school, college, or the pros. She was afraid he would get hurt.

Joseph Forte, 1999-2001

Talk about somebody who could shoot it! From the moment he played his first game as a freshman, he was one of the smoothest shooters Carolina has ever had. He could score from the three-point line, but what made him different was that he could also shoot it from midrange. He was almost a throwback in that way. You have to wonder what getting caught up in the coaching change did to his career. One more season in Chapel Hill would have been a big benefit for him.

Tyler Hansbrough, 2005-09

Think about how hard he worked and how good he was. But was he the most physically talented player Carolina has ever had? I don't think so. It makes you wonder about some of those who did have the raw talent.

I never saw Tyler get flustered. When he got knocked down, which was often, I used this as my indicator: how quickly he got off the floor determined how mad he was. When Gerald Henderson knocked him down at the Smith Center in 2007, he got up very fast. Carolina's Dewey Burke restrained him, which might have saved him on that night, because Tyler looked like he was ready to kick butt.

It was refreshing to see him act his age in Detroit when his team won the national championship. For four years, he had been so mature. It was great for him to enjoy it like a kid.

Brendan Haywood, 1997-2001

He was one of Carolina's all-time best shot blockers and a part of the 2000 Final Four team. Of course, that Final Four team also wore those jerseys with the interlocking NC logo on the front. That was unfortunate.

Antawn Jamison, 1995-98

Walter Davis, cool in everything he did, was probably the king in that category. But Antawn Jamison was not far behind. I've never seen a player catch the ball in a shooting motion like he did. His quintessential game was the home win over Duke in 1998, when he had the ball in his hands for less than a minute total but still shot 14 of 20 from the field and scored 35 points.

He was and is a genuinely nice person. I never saw him act like he was in a hurry or bothered by fans. If a player can be called a gentleman, he is a gentleman.

Bobby Jones, 1971–74

He was so quiet when he was at Carolina. When he got on the court, he was all about playing any way he could that would help win the game. He never looked for any credit. I thought he was an excellent all-around player, but I'm not sure I realized how good he was going to be at the next level and that he would develop into one of the elite players of his era.

In the 1973 ACC Tournament, Carolina lost to Wake Forest on a long frontcourt pass. Coach Smith was in the hallway talking to a reporter after the game as Bobby was leaving the arena. He interrupted his conversation with the writer to tell Bobby, "I was really pleased with how hard you played and how hard you tried to help us win the game." Bobby told me later it meant a lot to him that Coach Smith recognized his effort.

Michael Jordan, 1981–84

After his rookie season with the Bulls, Michael came back to Chapel Hill and did *ACC Hotline* with me. We played the clip of him in the 1983 Virginia game, when he stole the ball from Rick Carlisle and finished it with a dunk. Michael said, "I think that was the best game I ever played at Carolina. I did a little bit of everything in that game. I scored, rebounded, and played defense. I did what I needed to do to help the team win." Here was a guy who won a national championship, and he was saying that coming from 16 points down to beat Virginia was his best game. But looking at the highlights of that game, I don't think I could disagree with him. During that eight-and-a-half-minute comeback, he was terrific.

Mitch Kupchak, 1972–76

I really liked him, and I hate that his playing career ended with a serious injury.

He tells a terrific story about going into surgery in Chapel Hill. Neither of his parents was there, he was from Brentwood, New York, and he barely knew any of the doctors. He was feeling a little alone as the staff prepared to give him the anesthesia. And then he looked up, and Coach Smith was standing at the end of the bed with all the operating scrubs on. Mitch still gets emotional talking about it. "That's why you come play for him," he says.

He was a player who really appreciated his time at Carolina. I still remember pulling out of Dayton after the 1976 NCAA Tournament loss to Alabama. The bus was so full that there wasn't enough room for everybody. There sat Mitch Kupchak, a senior who had just played his last game, sitting in the aisle on top of someone else's bag, and he was so emotional about his Carolina career being finished.

Tommy LaGarde, 1973–77

In 1977, he had the unfortunate broken leg. Coach Smith later said he thought Carolina was the best team in the country that season. That was one of only two times I ever heard him say that. The other was in 1982. Tommy was one of those players you didn't really appreciate until you looked at the stat sheet.

Ty Lawson, 2006–09

When the referees threw the ball up, he was ready to play every single time. People acted like he was a problem sometimes, but I never saw that. I do know this: Carolina wouldn't have beaten LSU in the second round in 2009 without him, and there would have been no national championship in that scenario. How fortunate was Carolina to have two competitors like Felton and Lawson almost back to back?

George Lynch, 1989-93

Carolina wouldn't have won the 1993 national championship without him, not only because he was a terrific player both as a scorer and rebounder but because he took over that team and served as the leader. To this day, if a Carolina fan says, "I wish this team had a George Lynch on the floor," everyone knows immediately what that fan is talking about.

The drive to the '93 title had countless examples of him taking over as a leader. There's a famous photo taken from behind, where he has his arm around Eric Montross. It looks like two teammates who couldn't possibly be getting along better. What few people know is a couple minutes before that photo was taken, Lynch had jumped on Montross for not stopping a drive to the basket. Eric reminded him that he had four fouls, and that photo was taken as George accepted responsibility for his mistake. Not many players are willing to do that in the heat of an important game.

Sean May, 2002-05

He had some of the best hands for a big man that I have ever seen. I don't recall ever seeing him fumble an entry pass. When a player threw it to him in the paint, there was no question about whether he could handle the pass. He got on an incredible roll over the final month of the 2004–5 season. He was big-time in so many important games in that stretch, including the championship win over Illinois.

Bob McAdoo, 1971-72

He fouled out relatively early in the Final Four against Florida State in 1972, and it was difficult for that team to come back without him.

I've been impressed that even though he played only one year at Carolina, he has made a conscious effort to be part of the fabric of the program. When Carolina honored its living Hall of Fame members at a halftime ceremony, he came for the presentation even though he was an assistant coach with the Miami Heat, which had a game that same night. He flew in, did the halftime event, and then flew back for the game. He has always seemed appreciative of what Carolina did for him.

Rashad McCants, 2002-05

He could really shoot the basketball. I think it speaks to Roy Williams's coaching ability that they were able to coexist for two seasons. Many times, Coach Williams has referenced the fact that his staff thought his first year at Carolina might have been his best coaching job. It was one of the only times he ever had to coach a team with personalities he hadn't assembled himself. Recruiting is so important to him, and he is interested in off-the-court qualities as well as basketball skills.

Eric Montross, 1990-94

Eric took as much physical punishment in the paint as anyone who has ever played for Carolina. One night, I asked him, "Eric, why don't you just clean out that lane one time, and you'll have those guys off your back forever?"

He looked at me without smiling and said, "I wasn't coached that way in high school, and Coach Smith hasn't coached me that way." To him, it was pretty simple. He made it clear he wasn't going to do anything dirty.

I sat with him in the locker room in New Orleans after the national championship in 1993. I told him, "You did something tonight that will be with you for the rest of your life and even after your life is over. The day they carry your obituary in the paper, it will say, 'Eric Montross, a member of the 1993 national champions.'" He indicated he had not thought of it that way.

Mike O'Koren, 1976-80

He played in the era when it was possible to get a little closer to the players, and we had him to our home on occasion. I really liked the way he played. It didn't matter where you played him on the court because he could beat you from anywhere. He was from Jersey City and was one of the first players I got close to who helped me understand what players from the New York City area had to go through in order to develop a reputation and make it to college.

Sam Perkins, 1980–84

He was one of the best. He quietly got it done every single night. When the game finished, you'd think, *Sam didn't have a great night.* Then you'd look at the box score, and he had 16 points and 10 rebounds. I had no idea he would have such a long NBA career. He made himself into a great player.

J. R. Reid, 1986–89

He had a tremendous freshman season and was even on the cover of *Sports Illustrated*. His combination of speed and power was unusual for that era. Of course, he was also famous for some of his off-court exploits, including his antics with his cohort, Steve Bucknall. He had a successful pro career and has come back to a couple of the recent reunions. He's about to start breaking into broadcasting with Raycom.

Kenny Smith, 1983–87

If it hadn't been for LSU's John Tudor, who hacked Kenny on a break-away and broke his wrist, Carolina might have won the national championship in 1984. Even as a freshman, he had a knack for getting things done and keeping everyone involved. I would have liked to see a race from baseline to baseline between Kenny Smith, Ty Lawson, Raymond Felton, and Dexter Strickland. They might have been the fastest players with the ball who I covered.

Jerry Stackhouse, 1993–95

It's a shame that Jeff Capel's half-court shot in the 1995 game at Duke gets more attention than Jerry's dunk. That was one of the most physical, athletic plays I ever saw. It was also the only time I ever saw Jerry posture after a big play. He was usually stoic on the court, but he realized right away he had done something special.

Rasheed Wallace, 1993–95

During an event at the Friday Center one year, I moderated a discussion with Dean Smith and Tom Osborne. A member of the audience brought up Rasheed and basically talked about how difficult it had to be to deal with him. Coach Smith said, "I have never had one problem with Rasheed Wallace. All he wants to know is what you want him to do, and he tries to do it."

Rasheed's mother once told me she had a theory about all his technical fouls in the NBA. She said when she raised him, she would tell him what he had done wrong before she punished him. She thought maybe he got upset with the referees because they didn't give him an explanation. There might be some truth to that.

I've heard Coach Smith say Rasheed was one of the most talented players he ever had at Carolina. When he got it going, you just wanted to stand back and watch.

Donald Williams, 1991-95

I thought of him as a silent assassin. He didn't talk much. He had to go through an adjustment period because he was from nearby Garner and tremendous expectations were placed on him. But in that championship year of 1993, he didn't have to talk. He was terrific. There were a couple plays during that postseason when he pulled up from 20 feet and I thought to myself, *No!* Then he'd knock the bottom out of it.

Al Wood, 1977-81

One of the best individual efforts I ever saw was his 39-point game against Virginia in the national semifinals in 1981. That was a matchup of two of the best teams in the country. The Cavaliers had already beaten Carolina twice that season. Al basically decided he wasn't going to let that happen again. He was so good that night, it made the hair stand up on your arms.

As a person, he was always impressive, and he remains so today.

James Worthy, 1979-82

He was mature beyond his years as a person and a player. He overcame a serious injury his freshman year and went on to become one of the 50 greatest players in the first 50 years of the NBA.

It bothers me when he doesn't get the credit he deserves for the 1982 team. Michael made the shot that provided the winning margin. But that was James's team.

Dennis Wuycik, 1969-72

He was awfully good. His dad was such a huge fan that he would rig up a cassette player to his radio so he could record the broadcasts and go back and listen to what we said about Dennis.

Sometimes, I wonder if Carolina fans don't remember him as fondly as they should because of his later involvement with the ACC *Poop Sheet*, which sometimes printed unflattering things about the basketball program. It was unusual for a player who had been in the program to speak out on that subject.

Index

8 points in 17 seconds, 71-72, 74

Agnes, Miss, 176
Alexander, Ben, 183
Angell, Jones, 56, 115, 197, 203, 206, 210
Arnold, Bill, 65-66
Appenzeller, Herb, 46

Baddour, Dick, 129, 154-55, 158, 171, 192, 198, 203, 206
Baldwin, Buddy, 186
Barnes, Harrison, 55, 203
Barnes, Octavus, 169
Barth, Casey, 196
Barth, Connor, 149, 196
Bell, Mickey, 186
Black, Jimmy, 86
Bowen, Dr. Carl, 37
Bowen, Carroll, 67
Bowen, Harold, 67
Bradley, Dudley, 36
Brown, Larry, 158
Brown, Mack, 94, 120-22, 127-30, 167-70
Bryant, Kelvin, 51
Bucknall, Steve, 152
Bunting, John, 65-66, 95, 131, 149, 172-73

Capps, Jimmy, 30
Chesley, C.D., 46, 52-53, 58
Clark, Rusty, 55
Copeland, Mike, 182
Croom, Fred, 31-32
Crowell, Frank, 32
Crum, Dick, 24, 51, 69-70, 108, 131
Cunningham, Bubba, 135, 203, 213
Currie, Bill, 16, 62, 64, 66-67

Davenport, Oscar, 97
Davis, Butch, 95, 118, 131, 175, 189-91, 194
Davis, Greg, 168
Davis, Hubert, 61
Davis, Walter, 8-9, 71, 74, 101
Dedmon, Lee, 58
Denny, Jeff, 185
Doherty, Matt, 86, 96, 158-63, 172
Donnan, Jim, 170-71
Dooley, Bill, 63-66, 69
Driesell, Lefty, 157
Durham, Jean, 10-11, 19, 25, 63, 107, 112, 117, 135, 137, 198
Durham, Taylor, 11, 98, 124, 137-42, 145-47, 198
Durham, Wes, 11, 98, 116, 137-41, 142-45, 148, 198, 205-6

Elam, Johnny, 90
Ellington, Wayne, 183, 187

Fedora, Larry, 213
Fiddleman, Eric, 67
Fogler, Eddie, 83, 144, 173
Ford, Phil, 9, 73, 96, 152, 159
Forte, Joseph, 162
Fox, Rick, 61
Frasor, Bobby, 182, 186
Fuchs, Jeff, 119

Ginyard, Marcus, 182, 187
Green, Danny, 182
Guthridge, Bill, 71, 95-96, 152, 155, 157-58

Hansbrough, Tyler, 4, 10, 181-82, 186, 188
Hall, Jared, 149
Harland, Dr. James, 33
Harrison, Bill, 11
Harville, Charlie, 52, 56

Heavner, Jim, 86, 90, 100-101, 191
Holland, Terry, 79
Holliday, Bob, 24, 36, 108
Hooker, Michael, 154-55
Huggins, Vic, 32-33

Jones, Bobby, 8, 73
Jones, Trase, 196
Jordan, Michael, 3, 77-78, 82-83, 85-86, 87
Justice, Charlie: 1948 win over Texas, 125; and his teammates, 87-89, 91-92; as a radio analyst, 89-90; early memories, 14-15

Karl, George, 53
Keldorf, Chris, 169
Kennedy, John F., 45-46
Kirschner, Steve, 4, 203
Koury, Maurice, 131-33
Kupchak, Mitch, 74, 100
Kupec, Matt, 108, 154

Lawrence, Amos, 24, 69
Lawson, Ty, 183, 187
Lebo, Jeff, 152, 182, 187
Lewis, Bob, 55
Lotz, John, 173
Lunsford, Greg, 119
Lynch, George, 115, 136

Manuel, Jackie, 180
Maultsby, Mary, 30
McGuire, Frank, 35, 43, 44, 53, 81, 92
Miller, Larry, 55
Mixon, Mick, 104-7, 115, 136
Montgomery, John, 202
Montross, Eric, 186, 197

O'Koren, Mike, 10-11, 95
Okulaja, Ademola, 187

Osborne, Tom, 69

Packer, Billy, 60
Phelps, Derrick, 136
Presson, Jake, 26, 38-39, 41
Previs, Steve, 53-54

Quigg, Joe, 92, 123-24
Quincy, Bob, 68

Reeve, Ray, 16
Reid, J.R., 152
Rice, Homer, 62-63
Rice, King, 61, 157
Richardson, Jerry, 108-9
Rogers, Dave, 45
Ronald McDonald House, 133-35
Rosenbluth, Lennie, 4, 10, 92-94
Russell, Nealson, 40

Sampson, Ralph, 79-80
Scott, Charles, 54-55
Scott, Stuart, 4
Simmons, Brian, 168
Smith, Dean, 9, 11-12, 63, 131, 133; 1982 championship, 83-85; becoming UNC head coach, 43-44; comeback against Duke, 71; early work with, 72-73; film study, 178-80; relationship with Bob Knight, 76; relationship with John Thompson, 80, 154; retirement announcement, 150-55; strategy against Ralph Sampson, 79-80; taking over for McGuire, 35; travel, 100-104; win over Oklahoma in 1990, 61; Woody's first contact with, 42-43
Smith, Wade, 30-31
Sobba, Gary, 175, 198
Spurling, James, 109
Stackhouse, Jerry, 166
Steinbacher, Rick, 135
Streater, Steve, 51

Tatum, Jim, 31
Taylor, Lawrence. 70-71
Thacker, Jim, 58-59
Thorp, Holden, 193
Tilley, Greg, 67
Torbush, Carl, 94, 114, 170-72
Tudor, Caulton, 36

Valvano, Jim, 81

Walker, Bracey, 176
Ward, Ashby, 45
Warren, Greg, 149
Webb, Toby, 17-20
Weiner, Art, 14
WFMY, 45-50, 55-56
Willard, Ken, 34
Williams, Donald, 166
Williams, Roy: 96, 103, 111; 100 years
   of Carolina basketball, 4, 6-9; 2005 ti-
tles, 181, 186; 2009 titles, 182-83, 188;
2009-10 season, 184; as an assistant,
173-75, 177-78; as head coach, 178-81;
at Woody's retirement press conference,
203; on calling timeouts, 34; on keeping
things in house, 160-61; on replacing
Dean Smith, 155, 158; taking the Caro-
lina job, 165
Withers, Everett, 194
Wood, Al, 9, 11, 140
Woodruff, Bob, 116-17
Worthy, James, 77, 79, 82-83, 86
Wynn, Boss, 34

Yates, T.J., 201, 216

Zeugner, Jody, 67